Competencies at Work

Competencies at Work

Providing a Common Language for Talent Management

Bruce Griffiths and Enrique Washington

BEP BUSINESS EXPERT PRESS

First published in 2015 by
Business Expert Press, LLC
222 East 46th Street, New York, NY 10017
www.businessexpertpress.com
ISBN-13: 978-1-63742-327-1 (hardcover)
ISBN-13: 978-1-60649-968-9 (paperback)
ISBN-13: 978-1-60649-969-6 (e-book)

Business Expert Press Human Resource Management and Organizational Behavior Collection

Collection ISSN: 1946-5637 (print)
Collection ISSN: 1946-5645 (electronic)

Cover and interior design by Exeter Premedia Services Private Ltd., Chennai, India

First edition: 2015

10 9 8 7 6 5 4 3 2 1

To organizational leaders and talent management professionals who are committed to selecting and growing talented people.

Abstract

Competencies at Work will equip readers to understand, build, and implement competency models as a foundational and integrating element in talent management systems. Readers will understand how competency models have evolved to be the current best practice in defining criteria for all talent management applications such as selection interviews, promotion panels, assessment centers, job descriptions, and learning objectives. Specific guidance is provided in the steps needed to establish a sustainable model, with research results on universal competencies contained in most contemporary models. Also discussed are the challenges and issues in building and implementing models, such as the need for proof of efficiency and effectiveness, that is, reliable measures of competence and proof of validity. Competency models will be placed in the greater context of the complete talent management system needed to effectively recruit, select, orient, train, appraise, reward, motivate, and promote high-performing employees. The most popular competency applications of interviewing, assessment centers, survey-guided development, job modeling, and training criteria are specifically explored and explained. Finally recent case studies bring competencies to life in real organizational settings. Questions for reflection will help readers review and summarize important content in each chapter.

Keywords

assessment, behaviors, business, communications, competency, development, feedback, individual, leaders, leadership, learning, management, model, motivation, organization, organizational, performance, personal, process, role, skills, success, talent

Contents

Acknowledgments

I am a part of all I've met, and my contributions to this book represent an aggregate of 40 years of work experiences rubbing elbows with, and learning from, many, many excellent professionals; far too many for individual acknowledgment here. I must recognize, however, our initial editor, and my better half, Gail Walraven (an accomplished author in her own right) for her tireless support, many creative insights, and multiple improvements to our original manuscript. Thank you again Gail for all you do, and for being my best friend. I must also recognize my brother Keith Griffiths, a successful journalist and publisher, for his initial reading of the manuscript and for his several insightful suggestions that greatly improved the final product. I also want to acknowledge and thank my coauthor, colleague, and comrade Enrique Washington for his contributions and for his warm and generous spirit. Enrique you are the exemplar for the competency *Relationship Building* and it's a pleasure to know and work with you.

Bruce Griffiths

I have been blessed with experiences that have offered me amazing opportunities to learn and grow as a person and a professional. These experiences have made this achievement possible. I would like to acknowledge my coauthor, Bruce Griffiths; you have broadened my knowledge of evidence-based talent practices for my professional growth. You are a true mentor, friend, and colleague. I thank Gail Walraven, you went above and beyond to read and edit our manuscript. Because of your hard work and commitment to excellence, we were able to present a quality product. A big thank you to HMH for helping us with our graphics. Your work is amazing and you have been a great strategic partner. I am indebted to my friends and colleagues; you have been invaluable and gracious of your time, counsel, and support. There are so many of you that it would take more than a page to list you all. Thank you!

Thanks got to my amazing siblings, Stephanie, Erica, Monica, Euna, and Christa; you have always provided me with love and support. Thank you family! My deepest thanks to my wife Gretchen; you have been an amazing supporter and allowed me to live out my dreams of being an author. Without you and your unconditional love this book would not be possible. I would like to thank my children, Leo and Jill, you remind me each day of my blessings.

Lastly, I would like to acknowledge my Mom and Dad, who provided me with the foundation of patience, faith, and belief in myself. Your presence and sprit has been with me during every step of writing this book. Above all, you have taught me that with God all things are possible.

Enrique Washington

Foreword

As I sit down to write this foreword, I can't help but reflect on the history of Paymaster to Personnel to Human Resources to Human Capital Management. Quite a journey for the HR profession, and the last two iterations in the evolution of our science and discipline have been catalyzed by the advent of sophisticated and elegant competency modeling techniques. However the operative words here are technique and science. There are too many attempts by organizations to rush to design and develop their own competency model without rigor and methodologically correct approach. Though well-intended as this may seem, it does diminish the utility and successful application of these, often, incomplete and inexact models. That said, and even in light of so many lay practitioners trying hard to create the wheel, competencies have become table stakes if a company is to be great or remain great. Griffiths and Washington have provided the magic ingredient to help realize the true potential of competency models and their creation. Their approach is both elegant and practical. Their explanations of the science behind modeling and true stories that highlight the why and how provide even the least experienced layman the opportunity to learn and grow while helping to create a competitive advantage for their respective companies. But most importantly, a well-crafted competency model finds that special line of best fit by serving both the needs of the organization and the personal goals of the individual. A well designed and integrated model will truly have something for everyone by creating that common language of performance and potential. Hats off to Bruce and Enrique for so successfully addressing a long overdue need in such an elegant way!

Jeffrey M. Cava
EVP, CHRO
Starwood Hotels and Resorts World Wide, Inc.

Board of Directors
Society for Human Resource Management (SHRM)

Introduction

Are Competencies Important?

Let us begin with a common hiring scenario. After a recent resignation, your organization is interviewing for a new operations manager. The decision makers assemble to compare notes on the candidates they have interviewed. "I think Susan has the right stuff for this position," one says. "She was poised and radiated confidence when I asked difficult questions." Another speaks up: "I think John fits the bill. He's energetic and really seems to be a people person." A third interviewer prefers Bill because of his "street smarts and technical knowledge."

These opinions are weak because the interviewers are all looking for different qualities. They lack an understanding of what it really takes to manage and lead effectively. Nor do they have a common vocabulary to support a valid debate. The ensuing discussion is likely to become an unproductive test of wills as the interviewers lobby for their favorite candidate. To prove this point, imagine asking the interviewers to independently record and then share their definition of effective leadership. Chances are you will get as many answers as there are interviewers. Never fear, though, there is a solution to this confusion.

Over time, our definitions of what constitutes the *right stuff* for defining talent have evolved; the accepted standard is now the language of *competencies*. A single competency is defined as a cluster of behaviors representing one facet of what is needed to perform a job. For example, *Composure* is frequently cited as a personal competency that is important to many positions. A cluster of behaviors that demonstrate composure include showing patience, responding calmly to stressful circumstances, and demonstrating control of emotions. Having, and using, this kind of common vocabulary is especially vital in judging candidates for complex, cognitive jobs such as managing and leading.

This core concept of a *behavioral* characterization of a facet of competence has been fundamental to the language of competency since someone first articulated the notion that the best predictor of future behavior is past behavior (especially more recent behavior in a similar context).

Here is the basic idea: How much do you really care about what candidates tell you about their underlying motivation, values, attributes, and even training, compared to how they express these through their accomplishments and performance? How much can we really know about what is going on beneath the surface, compared to what we see in their current and recent actions?

And, of course, competent people are *the* essential factor in successful and enduring organizations. Without them, organizations are only empty buildings and idle machines. People have the ideas, and produce, market, and sell the organization's goods and services. Only people can organize and energize the enterprise. But what defines their competence? Is it raw talent? Knowledge? Skill? Ability? Personality? Motivation?

This book will explore this relatively new, but now widely accepted, concept of competency and competency models. It will argue that these models are absolutely essential in providing a common language for talent management across human resource systems. Indeed, without an accepted model of the ideal employee, individual talent systems (e.g., recruiting, hiring, promoting, training, appraising) are suboptimized and may even contradict each other.

The pages that follow will provide a clear, best-practice definition of competence that emphasizes effective *behavior* and *performance* as a primary definitional element. Building and implementing models will be presented, as will sample competencies and complete models. Case studies of successful applications in organizations will demonstrate the efficacy of competency models. Finally, nuances in presentation and interpretation of models in the key talent areas of selection, training, and performance management will be discussed.

It is important to note a legal reason for learning about competency models. Legally defensible selection and promotion systems must be based on valid criteria. Spending time on ensuring a valid model helps provide assurance that any organizational evaluation is reliable and valid.

It is also important to point out what this book does not include. Our focus is on the elements and systems that ensure that an organization is staffed by exceptional individuals capable of producing needed results in their defined roles. Once onboard and fully functioning, their retention and motivation are part of other human resource systems that ensure lasting tenure and continuing interest. These systems include compensation, benefits, performance management (appraisal), engagement, employee (labor) relations, safety, employee assistance programs, and others. These are certainly important in overall management of an enterprise, but detailed description is beyond the scope of this book.

Finally, here are some specifics on our target reader. Whether you are a small service business with fewer than a dozen associates or a global giant doing business around the world, we hope that this book will help you understand and be able to create and implement a competency model to provide the criteria needed for essential decisions and actions to optimize your most valuable resource: the human resource.

CHAPTER 1

The Underlying Principles of Competency Modeling

This chapter will provide a fundamental understanding of the *why*, *what*, and *how* of competency modeling. Let us start with the observation that all organizations have a very practical need to identify the criteria that define their ideal employee. Any leader who makes decisions about whom to hire, whom to promote, what skills to train, or how to appraise, implicitly assumes this ideal criteria. Defining this *model employee*—and creating a blueprint to replicate him or her—is an ongoing challenge dating back thousands of years. Indeed, two millennia ago the Chinese bureaucracy identified its *ideal* member as someone who could pass rigorous tests on the *six arts* of arithmetic, writing, music, archery, culture, and horsemanship.

Competencies are now the most prevalent method used to define ideal employees and have become a fundamental part of talent management systems across organizations. Talent management has been defined by the Society for Human Resources Management as "the implementation of *integrated* strategies or systems designed to increase workplace productivity by developing improved processes for attracting, developing, retaining and utilizing people with the required skills and aptitude to meet current and future business needs" (emphasis added). Therefore, having a competency-based system to link these processes is the key to cohesive and effective talent management.

Historical Influences on Current Competency Constructs

Modern concepts of an ideal employee have roots in the assessment center movement, dating back to World War II. For hiring and promotion, assessment centers created behavioral definitions of competence, calling them *dimensions* or *variables* and then used simulations to test the readiness of candidates. This methodology, used first at the Office of Strategic Services (OSS, now the CIA) and then at the Bell System (now AT&T), created a better and more predictable way to select spies as well as supervisors.[1]

Because assessment centers relied on the real-time observance of performance in simulations, evaluators needed to reference very specific behaviors to allow reliable ratings. (For example, *Presentation Skills* could be broken down into behaviors such as eye contact, gestures, loudness, organization, and inflection). These behavior-based definitions were excellent in providing an efficient and effective method of review and propelled the popularity of this form of evaluation.

Over time, other talent management professionals were interested in more holistic views of the employee and generated specific job requirements based on the knowledge, skills, abilities, and other characteristics (referred to within the human resources profession as KSAOs) needed to perform well in a particular role. KSAOs could be used to define roles, and in a training context, provide learning objectives that could be framed in terms of knowledge gained or skills acquired (assuming that the individual had the required ability). Career counselors added values and motives to the mix as relevant variables when discussing potential positions and paths.[2]

The term *competency* really entered the talent management lexicon in 1973 when noted American psychologist David McClelland wrote the pivotal paper "Testing for Competence Rather than for Intelligence."[3] It was further popularized by McClelland's colleague, Richard Boyatzis, and others who used the competency concept in the context of performance improvement.

Another influence on the evolution of modern competency modeling was Dr. Malcolm Knowles, and his seminal work in adult education and lifelong learning. Focused on what he called *andragogy* (i.e., adult learning versus pedagogy: childhood learning) Dr. Knowles referred to *competencies* as necessary segmentations in describing what was needed to perform in overall complex and cognitive leadership and life roles.[4] He noted that in order to facilitate learning it was absolutely necessary

Table 1.1 Malcolm Knowles' original worker competencies

Worker competencies
Career planning
Using technical skills
Accepting supervision
Giving supervision
Getting along with people
Cooperating
Planning
Delegating
Managing

to parse broad learning agendas such as teaching *leadership* into component parts such as *Communications Skills* or *Delegating*. In his listing of needed *worker competencies*, one can see the beginnings of several modern universal competencies such as *Organizing and Planning* and *Relationship Building* (see Table 1.1).

While not working directly in the corporate world of selection and development Dr. Knowles distinguished reputation, and his independent and simultaneous use of the term competency provided credibility and acceptance.

A final competency influence came from the worlds of personality and trait research and the paper-and-pencil (now mostly online) testing associated with them. Thousands of individual tests were developed to measure hundreds of various cognitive and social constructs such as intelligence, personality traits, values, attitudes, and beliefs. For example, one of the world's most popular personality instruments, the Myers–Briggs Type Indicator, measures, among other things, an individual's personality preference for extroverted or introverted behaviors. Another is the Watson–Glaser test, which measures critical thinking and is correlated with general intelligence. This entire body of testing knowledge creates an additional, very comprehensive resource to help explain underlying influences on behavior.

Defining Competencies Today

Despite lingering debate around definitions,[5] professionals concur that a *competency* serves to connect these various influences into a single construct, with the "primary definitional element being a behavioral or performance description."[6] Thus an *individual competency* describes a specific set of behaviors or performance indicators associated with a facet of exceptional performance in an organizational role. Each competency reflects a unique combination of knowledge, skills, abilities, and other factors that are driven and influenced by multiple traits and motivations, ultimately manifesting themselves in skillful behavior. A *competency model* refers to a complete set, or collection, of different competencies that are applicable to a single organization, or more generically, to every organization. Ultimately, competence is manifested in explicit behaviors (what you do and *how you show up*) and *performance* (decisions, actions, and results); while *intent* and *potential* are part of the much more complex, and largely unseen, world of values, traits, and motivations (the O in KSAOs).

Active Listening is an example of a competency associated with many models. The definition includes behaviors such as eye contact, head nodding, verbal affirmations, smiles, and accurate paraphrasing or summarizing. How one is judged in this competency depends on knowing how to listen and also having the motivation to listen. (Do I value other people's opinions? Am I curious about their experiences and feelings?) And while active listening may be a globally applicable concept, the types of behavior that illustrate effective performance have a cultural context that must be factored into local behavioral definitions. For example, in some cultures listening is important, but looking directly at those in positions of higher authority is considered disrespectful. Figure 1.1 illustrates the visible and hidden elements in *Active Listening*.

Comprehensive competency models offer an integrating framework that provides an essential foundation for key human resources processes, offering a complete menu of dimensions that can be sorted for individual organizational roles and levels. Figure 1.2 shows one commercially available competency model that includes 41 competencies distributed into seven clusters.[7] This model presents a complete set of competencies that can be sorted by function and level in an organization.

Figure 1.3 is an example of a detailed definition of the *Active Listening* competency within the *Communications* cluster.

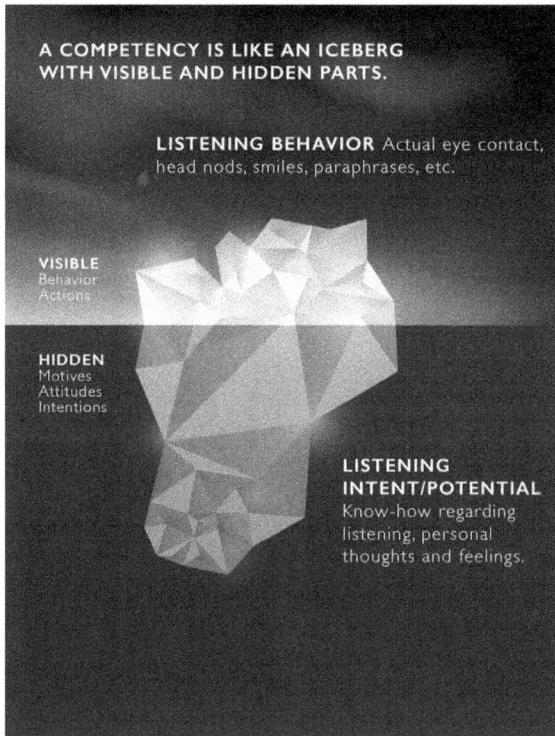

Figure 1.1 *A simple representation of the concept of a competency*

Issues to Consider When Developing Competency Models

Several issues need to be addressed to fully understand, and more importantly apply, any given competency model:

1. The need for reliable and valid models and measurements
2. The necessary complexity and need for context of any given model
3. The decision to define competencies in terms of behaviors or motives and traits
4. The number of competencies that should be included in a model
5. The equality or relative weight of any given competency.

The Need for Reliable and Valid Competency Models and Measurements

When developing criteria (and any accompanying test or measurement of that criteria) it is essential to insure that accepted thresholds of both

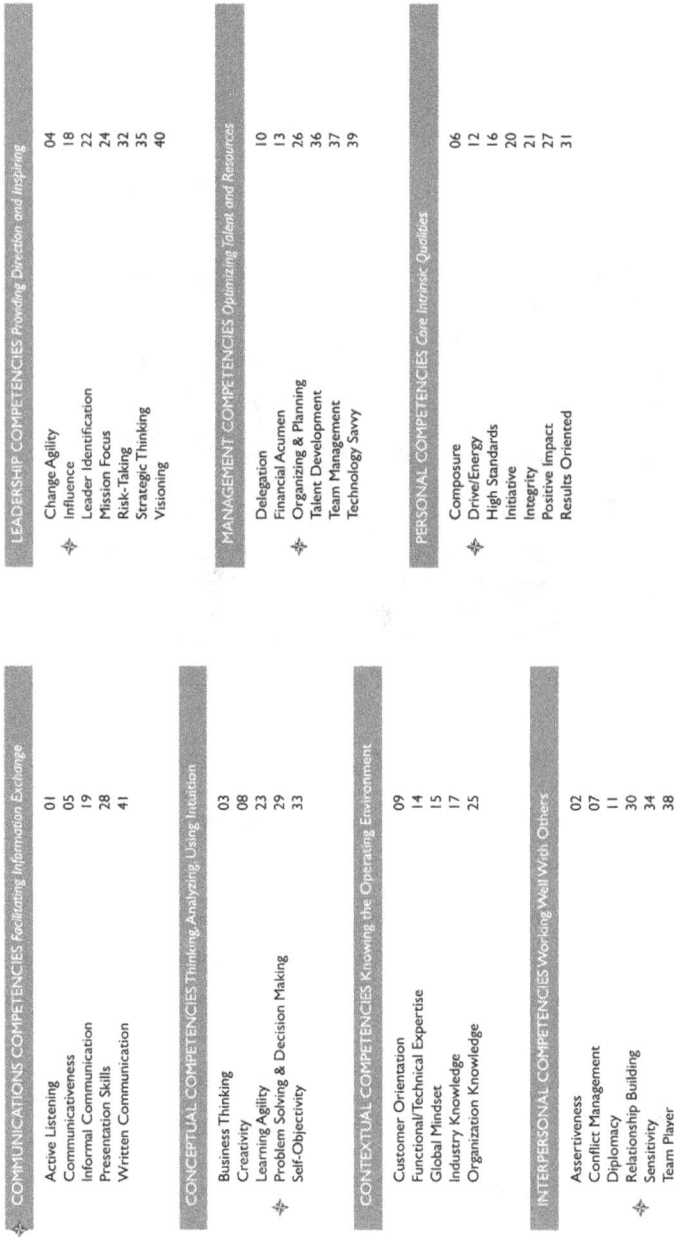

COMMUNICATIONS COMPETENCIES *Facilitating Information Exchange*

Active Listening	01
Communicativeness	05
Informal Communication	19
Presentation Skills	28
Written Communication	41

CONCEPTUAL COMPETENCIES *Thinking, Analyzing, Using Intuition*

Business Thinking	03
Creativity	08
Learning Agility	23
Problem Solving & Decision Making	29
Self-Objectivity	33

CONTEXTUAL COMPETENCIES *Knowing the Operating Environment*

Customer Orientation	09
Functional/Technical Expertise	14
Global Mindset	15
Industry Knowledge	17
Organization Knowledge	25

INTERPERSONAL COMPETENCIES *Working Well With Others*

Assertiveness	02
Conflict Management	07
Diplomacy	11
Relationship Building	30
Sensitivity	34
Team Player	38

LEADERSHIP COMPETENCIES *Providing Direction and Inspiring*

Change Agility	04
Influence	18
Leader Identification	22
Mission Focus	24
Risk-Taking	32
Strategic Thinking	35
Visioning	40

MANAGEMENT COMPETENCIES *Optimizing Talent and Resources*

Delegation	10
Financial Acumen	13
Organizing & Planning	26
Talent Development	36
Team Management	37
Technology Savvy	39

PERSONAL COMPETENCIES *Core Intrinsic Qualities*

Composure	06
Drive/Energy	12
High Standards	16
Initiative	20
Integrity	21
Positive Impact	27
Results Oriented	31

Figure 1.2 Universal competency model

Source: Based on the Polaris Competency Model© 2014 Organization Systems International

ACTIVE LISTENING

Effective performers offer their full attention when others speak. They listen actively, giving verbal and nonverbal cues of their interest. When the speaker has finished, they paraphrase what was said to ensure understanding.

EFFECTIVE PERFORMERS...

- ⇨ Attend fully when others speak.
- ⇨ Give cues of their interest.
- ⇨ Paraphrase and summarize.

TO WHAT EXTENT DOES THIS INDIVIDUAL...

- ⇨ Paraphrase or summarize to ensure understanding?
- ⇨ Give full attention without interrupting?

Individuals with **TOO LITTLE** of this competency can be perceived as...	Individuals with **TOO MUCH** of this competency can be perceived as...
⇨ Uncaring	⇨ Eavesdropping
⇨ Rude	⇨ Passive
⇨ Inattentive	⇨ Having no opinion

TIPS

- ⇨ It's not enough to listen, you should also communicate to the speaker that you're listening – show interest, give verbal and nonverbal cues that you're interested.
- ⇨ Eliminate distractions (e.g., phone, computer, tablet) and create a good listening environment when possible.

INTERVIEW QUESTIONS

- ⇨ Describe a time when you received negative feedback. How did it turn out?
- ⇨ Tell us about a time when you did not listen as well as you might have.

QUOTE

"Listen or your tongue will keep you deaf."

- Native American Proverb

Figure 1.3 Competency detail (Active Listening)

reliability and validity are met. This is especially important because models, and associated measurements, are typically used to select, appraise, and promote individuals and must be legally defensible. But even more importantly, measures of reliability and validity define how efficient and effective a measure is, and ultimately whether any investment in models and measurements is worthwhile.

Reliability means that a test or measure produces consistent individual results over time and from person to person. Validity means that a test accurately measures what it purports to measure—that is, it can be used to predict behavior. It follows that validity will be problematic for any measure that is not first reliable.

A simple example illustrates, and differentiates, these important concepts. A tape measure is a *reliable* measure of a person's height, providing consistent, repeatable data. Height can be a predictor of success in professional basketball (the average professional male basketball player is 6 ft 7 in tall, while the average American male is 5 ft 10 in). So a tape measure provides a reliable measure of height, which is a *valid* predictor of success (just one of many in this case). Many personality inventories that measure more abstract dimensions such as extroversion (being expressive and action-oriented) may seem valid for certain organizational roles, such as a salesperson. However, reliability research has shown that many of these instruments are inconsistent from one administration to the next. Individual results may change from day to day or be manipulated by the test taker because the test is transparent, and they are driven to pro-vide more socially desirable answers. This lack of reliability can invalidate much of the instrument's predictive power. Consequently, criteria (that is, a competency model) must be able to be both reliably measured *and* relevant (valid) to be useful in application.

Complexity and the Need for Context

Competency models are inherently complex because they reflect multi-faceted human behavior at work. While individual competencies attempt to isolate distinct performance factors, in practice they overlap and inter-act. This creates a level of ambiguity that must be expected and accepted. Individual competencies do not stand-alone; they necessarily dissect roles into smaller parts to gain a more useful understanding of what it takes to perform successfully.

When first presented with a competency model, users may resist being defined and sorted into different *boxes*—they believe they repre-sent more than just a sum of several dozen competencies (and they do!). Therefore, it is essential when using an entire competency model, to look at not just the parts, but also the whole, and the context for the whole. But, just as you cannot write a sentence without individual words (and the meaning of the sentence is more than just a jumble of the words), relevant competencies for any particular role need to be seen as a whole, synergistic with one another. For complete meaning, the competency set has to be put in the contexts of both the role and the general situation surrounding the role.

The concept of a *job model* is replacing the job description as the most important context for defining and using a subset of competencies.

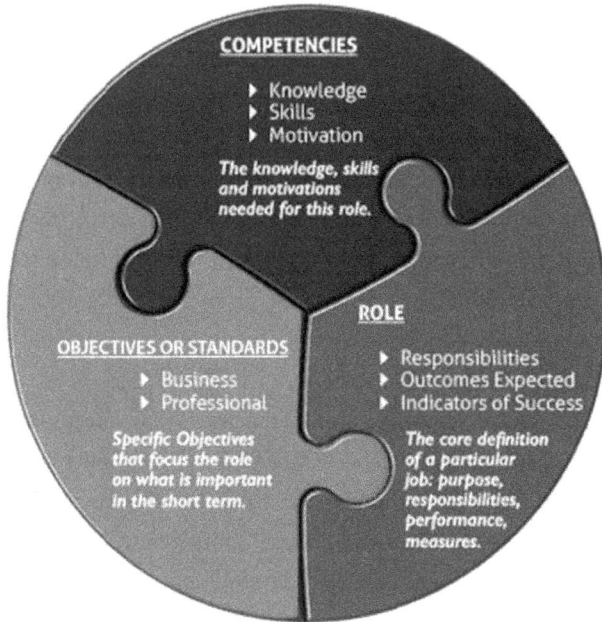

Figure 1.4 Complete job model

A job model places competencies in this context by combining needed competence with two other job components (objectives, standards, and responsibilities) for a more complete understanding of a particular role.

As illustrated in Figure 1.4, needed role clarity for any job is achieved when:

- Responsibilities are clear (including indicators of success and expected outcomes for each accountability);
- Objectives have been set, or clear standards have been communicated; and
- The subset of competencies needed to meet responsibilities and accomplish objectives is identified.

While organizations will have different formats for describing positions, it is important to place any competency model within this more complete representation of a job to help clarify, limit, and correctly apply relevant competencies.

Having a complete set of competencies (such as those listed in Figure 1.2) as an organizing structure can also help differentiate job analysis, job evaluation, and competency modeling. Job *analysis* focuses on the task, or the individual, to produce activity expectations or KSAOs for a particular job (or family of jobs) and often produces a classic position description with required knowledge and skills listings. Job *evaluation* is used to value a role for compensation purposes and takes into consideration factors such as scope (span of control), signature authority (budget responsibility), decision-making authority, and autonomy. External comparisons are often used to put the job in a salary range. *Competency models* go beyond individual jobs and provide a universal menu for all the roles in an enterprise.

In the article "Doing Competencies Well: Best Practices in Competency Modeling," Michael Campion and colleagues pay particular attention to differences between job analysis, evaluation, and competency modeling. They note a key difference: Competency models tend to be top-down, driven by organizational development, while job analysis and evaluation are bottom-up and more isolated from organizational strategy and goals.[8] Many practitioners have noticed that competency modeling projects are truly organizational development efforts, because they provide a top-down intervention that helps define the leadership behaviors desired; that is, they can help define the *culture* of the organization.

Defining Competencies in Terms of Behaviors or Motives

As previously mentioned, definitions of competencies can be ambiguous at times. Historically, some practitioners, such as assessment center advocates, prefer using behavioral descriptions while others, such as coaches or career counselors, favor traits or personality factors. In actual practice today, behaviors are preferred as they are more easily observed and measured, whereas traits and motives are myriad and hidden, and therefore more difficult to measure. Academic and research settings have also seemed to favor traits or personality dimensions for defining competence. Once again, most modern competency definitions have resolved this argument by including both behavior and the other factors such as personality and motivation.

Current science suggests that primary definitions are behavioral, but that other factors are included to allow a richer definition depending on context. In context, behavioral definitions can be most useful in predicting future performance (selection and placement), but underlying knowledge, skill, and other factors play a key role in developing competence. For example, the competency *Presentation Skills* (public speaking) provides a clear illustration of how motivation, knowledge, and skill interact to define competent performance. A young sales professional might receive the feedback that he or she needs to improve sales presentations to potential customers: *You seem nervous and become too wordy. You're very mechanical in delivery and the lack of enthusiasm diminishes your credibility.* With this feedback, the sales professional becomes motivated to learn the competence (a job requirement) and can gain knowledge regarding public speaking (read a good book on giving presentations), but ultimately he must practice the skill to perform and behave at a higher level (can join Toastmasters to practice, practice, and practice). The demonstrated skill becomes the true, practical, definition of competence. Along the way he or she might explore how other factors influence competence, for example, how personality helps and hinders. Being an introvert may result in reduced motivation to *be on stage* and that understanding can help reveal and reduce potential obstacles to skill acquisition.

This is also a good example of how in training, development, and career planning, the hidden variables (motives, values, attitude, beliefs, and personality) are important influencers of competence, representing the preferences, intent, or potential of an individual. So once again it is most useful to think of competence as skillful behavior that can be improved through knowledge acquisition or skill practice, and that can be influenced, energized, and kindled by appropriate motivations.

The Number of Competencies That Should Be Included in a Model

How many competencies are needed in a complete model? A restrictive approach will lead to fewer competencies, but requires that each competency cover a much broader range of behaviors and KSAOs. This makes it easier to explain and promote the competency model but harder, if not impossible, to use. A model with more competencies means that each competency is a more *specific* cluster of behaviors.

This results in a more complex model, but more accurately differentiates actual performance.

For example, a broader competency model that includes just a single, overall *Communications Skills* competency will be simpler as a representation, but will inevitably lead to confusion in evaluating the competency or providing individual feedback. An individual can have weak *Presentation Skills* but excel in *Written Communications*. If there was only one overall *Communications* competency how could one accurately rate this individual? Neither a high, low, or average score would accurately represent the individual's ability. A more useful alternative is to divide the competency into more specific categories such as *Presentation Skills*, *Informal (verbal) Communications*, *Written Skills*, and *Listening Skills*. These differentiated competencies allow for more reliable evaluation, productive feedback, and developmental planning. As described earlier, the rich history of assessment center evaluation provides plentiful proof of the need for this differentiation to produce acceptable consistency among raters.[9] In examining the commercial models available today, it appears that about three dozen independent competencies are required for a complete organizational menu.

The Equality or Relative Weight of Any Given Competency

Not all competencies are created equal. A shortfall in the competency *Integrity* may override exceptional competence across all other dimensions. Additionally, an organization's vision, mission, and values (key marketplace differentiators) will help determine, which competencies are most important to that organization. For example an organization differentiating itself with world-class customer service may require *Active Listening* and *Customer Orientation* as key competencies for every customer-facing role. Likewise matrix organizations may require much more competence in areas such as *Initiative, Assertiveness or Confidence*, and *Influence* to overcome a lack of formal authority.

To be successful in building and implementing a competency model, all the above considerations should be taken into account—and they also argue for rigorous orientation and training when first introducing the model.

How to Build and Customize a Competency Model

Various methods of job analysis and competency modeling have been developed over the years to inform competency definition and selection. The approaches listed below have been used individually or in concert with others to build and validate models in real organizational settings. The most rigorous approaches combine techniques to produce robust models.

High-Performer Interviews and Focus Groups

Interviews and focus groups with high performers are the centerpiece of most modeling processes. Interviews are conducted with exemplar individuals to identify the knowledge, skills, and abilities they possess that set them apart. High performers are classically identified as those individuals with a history of generating both results and respect. They are also likeable (a shorthand for emotional intelligence) and passionate about their work. A significant portion of the high-performer interview is dedicated to soliciting examples (or stories) of effective and ineffective performance, which are later used to provide *real life* illustrations of the competencies in use. For example, the following condensed story was provided by a high-performing company executive as an example of a *personal best*:

> I inherited a group of factories that were being milked for profit but needed dramatic investment. They were dirty and disorganized. I took pictures and a compelling financial case to corporate HQ and convinced the board we needed the investment. (It helped that I had blown up the pictures of these rust belt factories and posted them around the boardroom). I convinced them. After getting the needed resources I took the current management teams of the factories on a field trip to a sister division in Europe. This group of factories was clean and efficient. I meant this to be a trip to the future! It worked. We now run a model, profitable group of factories.

This type of anecdote is analyzed for the competencies it represents. In this case, on display are the proficiencies *Financial Acumen*, *Visioning*, *Problem Solving*, *Diplomacy*, *Influence*, and *Presentation Skills*.

Internal Document and Literature Review

Competency researchers often conduct an internal organizational review to identify existing resources that point to performance measures or benchmarks. For example, job descriptions, recruiting material, performance appraisal documents, and learning objectives can all provide inferences of competence. A variety of commercial organizations also provide examples of specific job competencies to purchase and use as a starting point.[10]

Competency Validation

Once a prototype competency list has been developed, it can be converted into a questionnaire and given to a representative sample of job content experts (that is, supervisors of the target role). Respondents are asked to rate how essential each competency is to successful performance from *not necessary* to *absolutely essential*. The results are statistically analyzed to validate each competency. This strategy, called *content validation*, is an accepted industry practice for defending the validity of a specific competency model.[11] Of course, studies that track the effectiveness of using competencies to predict future success provide the gold standard for legitimacy. These longitudinal studies test the validity of the model in actual organizational application. For example, assessment center ratings across relevant competencies are correlated with on-the-job measures of effectiveness such as performance appraisal ratings or actual business results. These scientific studies have proven the economic value of models and their measurements.[12]

Strategic Fit and Presentation

Because the modeling process typically looks backward in time (that is, draws from historical examples) there is some danger in *the tail wagging the dog*. This means the proposed competency model should be tested against the organization's future strategy and vision to ensure the competencies drive behavior toward a preferred future. This process can be more art than science, and a seasoned practitioner can provide insight to detect missing or incomplete competencies, with an eye to the future. Often such competencies are listed as *aspirational* and acquiring them becomes an overall organizational development effort.

Once completed, competency models can be presented to the organization as dictionaries, card decks, and one-page summaries (quick guides). Interestingly enough, even in this digital age, physical card decks have proven popular among the commercially available models as a preferred way of presenting the information. Each card is a separate competency and the decks can be sorted by individuals or teams to inform talent management applications.

Universal Competencies

While most competency models contain several dozen individual competencies, research has consistently surfaced a subset of competencies common to most well-respected models. One particularly robust report by W. Arthur and others analyzed a total of 34 articles that reported dimension (competency) level information and was able to collapse 168 assessment center dimension labels into an overriding set of six dimensions common to most effective leaders:[13]

1. Sensitivity: consideration and awareness of others
2. Communication skills
3. Drive
4. Influencing others
5. Organizing and planning
6. Problem solving

In addition to validation through solid research, these competencies also pass muster intuitively. Take a moment to personally identify an exceptional manager, or coworker, and then isolate the attributes that makes him or her more effective. You will likely identify an empathetic (*Sensitivity*), motivated (*Drive and Energy*), efficient (*Organizing and Planning*), and powerful (*Influence*) person who exercises good judgment (*Problem Solving and Decision Making*) and expresses herself well (*Communications Skills*). (See Chapter 4 regarding the *Big Six*.)

Competencies Across the Talent Pipeline

A complete organizational competency model includes all the competencies necessary to differentiate roles across the organization, from individual contributors adding value primarily through functional and technical competence, to general managers and company presidents who are exceptional because of their leadership competence. These universal models necessarily contain certain competencies that are only valid for particular levels in the talent pipeline. For example, a competency such as *Delegation* is not usually applicable unless the individual has someone to delegate to, that is, a direct report.

On the other hand, some competencies, such as *Informal Communications Skills*, may apply across all levels of a talent pipeline, although they may require increasing levels of proficiency as higher levels of responsibility are attained.

Figure 1.5 shows a generic representation of how a four-level talent pipeline interacts with and uses their competency model. It is useful to create custom versions of this for specific organizations, incorporating their language and specific characteristics.

Some competencies are likely to be less essential as the employee moves higher in the talent pipeline. An example is *Special Expertise*, a

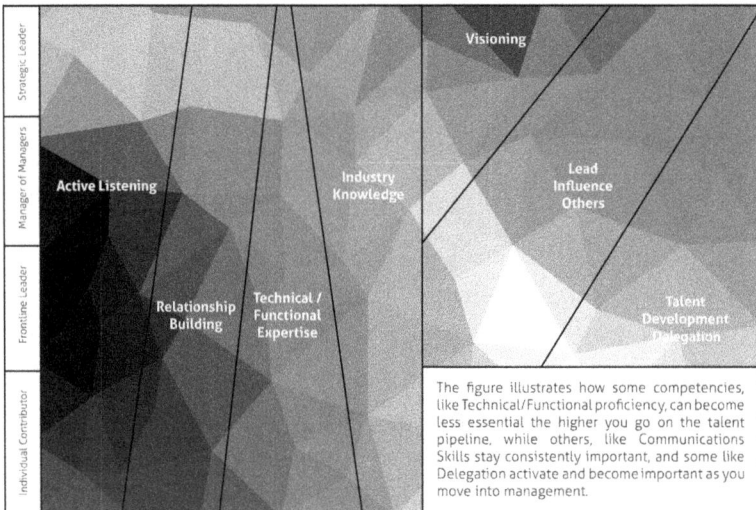

The figure illustrates how some competencies, like Technical/Functional proficiency, can become less essential the higher you go on the talent pipeline, while others, like Communications Skills stay consistently important, and some like Delegation activate and become important as you move into management.

Figure 1.5 Talent pipeline

functional or technical competence such as those found in software development, the law, accounting, or engineering. Others such as *Learning Agility* will likely retain their importance across all levels. And some, such as *Communications Skills*, can become more important as you climb the talent ladder. Of course, this is a general guideline—some positions, such as a key account sales representative or chief scientist, may require special competency combinations not necessarily correlated to their level on the talent ladder.

From the largest Fortune 500 conglomerates to the smallest business, the concepts of competency modeling provide a better way to define a job, hire the right people, evaluate them, and provide a clear path to develop their talents—all the while ensuring that there is a strategic fit with the goals and values of the organization.

A well-researched, well-presented, and validated competency model provides a common talent language across an organization. Competency models are a key to optimizing talent systems, and without this common language organizations risk making talent management processes inefficient and ineffective.

Questions for Reflection

1. How do competency models help integrate talent management systems?
2. How is competency best defined?
3. What are some of the challenges inherent in building, understanding, and applying competency models?
4. How can the competency modeling process be leveraged as an organizational development effort?
5. How can you prove a competency model is useful?
6. How do competencies interact with talent pipelines?

CHAPTER 2

A Single Competency Examined

Because every individual competency is a set of behaviors driven by a very complex combination of knowledge, skills, ability, and other factors, rarely can you completely comprehend a single competency with simply a one- or two-sentence description.

In this chapter, we are going to do a deep dive into one of the more complex, interpersonal competencies: *Assertiveness*. We have selected *Assertiveness* to put under the microscope because it has been singled out over decades in study after study as fundamental to effective performance in a wide range of roles.[1] While core definitions of *Assertiveness* have remained constant over the years, it has gone by many names including *Confidence*, *Ego*, *Self-Esteem*, *Independence*, and *Need for Approval*. But at its core, being appropriately *Assertive* is defined by the self-reliant behaviors needed to power persuasive communications, decisive action, and effective influence. *Assertiveness* is so important as a primary driver of success that classic assessment centers adopted the unusual scoring convention of negative scores for *both* ends of a five-point scoring continuum (more confidence was better but only up to a point). It was the only competency scored this way and candidates who were awarded lower scores (a 1 or a 2 on the scale) were evaluated as requiring too much peer or superior approval before acting (they lacked needed confidence), while those with higher scores (a 4 or a 5 on the scale) were rated as too independent and at risk of alienating others or ignoring better ideas, based on potential arrogance.

To help understand this complex competence, we are going to explore *Assertiveness* through three lenses: (1) we will look at the classic definitional elements of narrative and performance indicators; (2) we will examine *Assertiveness* through the perspective of degree of proficiency needed for varying roles or levels; and (3) we will explore it through a development lens; that is, how do I acquire needed *Assertiveness.*

Classic Definitional Elements

The following exploration of *Assertiveness* in one universal model presents all the needed ingredients in a basic understanding of the competency. It describes what appropriate confidence looks like, what organizational jeopardy you may be in without it, and what happens when a strength is overdone until it becomes a weakness. It also provides ready questions to help quiz potential job candidates on their *Assertiveness,* as well as suggesting items to assess *Assertiveness* in a job incumbent. Finally, it adds a quote to spice up the definition with a little expert wisdom.

Assertiveness

Definition

Effective performers readily offer opinions and take action even when their position may be unpopular. They are willing to challenge others appropriately when required. They are self-confident—they trust their own judgment and are not overly dependent upon the approval of others.[2]

Effective Performers

    a. Challenge others appropriately
    b. Willingly assert their point of view when required
    c. Are self-confident
    d. Trust their own judgment
    e. Are not overly dependent on the approval of others.

On the Job Assessment

To What Extent Does This Individual

    a. Confront others in a constructive fashion when necessary?
    b. Maintain personal convictions when faced with opposition?

Table 2.1 *The behavioral continuum—competence under-done and over-done*

Individuals with TOO LITTLE of this competency can be perceived as	Individuals with TOO MUCH of this competency can be perceived as
• Inactive • Submissive • Passive	• Arrogant • Aggressive • Insensitive

Tips and Miscellaneous Advice

Know the difference between being right and being righteous.
Watch for blind spots.
Balance objectivity with sensitivity.
Be willing to confront but remember to preserve the relationship.

Hiring Interview Questions

Describe a time when you had to take a stand against your peers or superiors.
Describe a work situation in which you lost confidence or were unsure of yourself.
What did you do? How did it work out?

Reflections

The basic difference between being assertive and being aggressive is how our words and behavior affect the rights and well-being of others.
—Sharon Anthony Bower

Degree of Proficiency Needed

To build a more complete understanding of a competency like *Assertiveness*, we can also include the escalating proficiency required at different levels, or for different roles, in an organization. One can think of the classic proficiency progression from apprentice, to journeyman, to master craftsman in order to help frame this perspective. This point of view recognizes the reality that the self-confidence necessary to be a sales manager may differ from that required for being a research assistant. From a career and growth perspective it also suggests that climbing the talent pipeline ladder will require increased competence and provides specifics on what that looks like.

The continuum presented in Table 2.2 shows *Assertiveness* across a four-level talent pipeline, with the addition of an *inadequate* level to contrast negative behaviors with proficient ones.

A proficiency continuum provides not only a needed perspective to understand competence at work, but also very useful tools for career planning, performance management, and selection. Ambitious employees can readily see what is required to move up in an organization, and managers can use the continuum as a guide to rate behavior and as *writing wizards* in performance appraisal narratives. Interviewers can gauge candidate responses to questions and match answers against required proficiency.

Development Perspectives

A final perspective in a complete understanding of *Assertiveness* is to view the competence through the vantage point of development. Most effective definitions include not only a perspective on development, but also a framework for improvement. What follows is an example of such a developmental guide for *Assertiveness*.

Development Guide for the Assertiveness Competency

Significance or Degree of Difficulty

One's ability to effectively assert a point of view is a major determinant of ultimate success. This competency is *Assertiveness*, and at its root is confidence—a fundamental trait that impacts all facets of life. In organizational contexts, it is a disservice if team members cannot confidently represent their expertise and opinions. Figure 2.1 illustrates how difficult it is to acquire this competency, based on extensive research in operational settings. Degree of difficulty influences whether you should hire candidates who lack the competency and then train them later, or instead choose to hire only those who already have the competency.

Table 2.2 Assertiveness proficiency continuum

Level	Performance indicators and behavioral episodes
4 Master or guru	• Models the executive self-assurance needed to project a positive organizational image in external forums • Communicates a clear, confident, and solid vision and purpose for the direction of the organization • Listens to others and gathers information, but decisively follows own judgment • Shows an appropriate conviction in the accuracy of own strategies and business decisions • Exudes utmost confidence in own vision and strategies; believes completely in personal ability to achieve goals
3 Exceptional or expert	• Has confidence and conviction based on experience and expertise • Confidently champions opinions and programs • Is comfortable when challenged in executive forums • Is not afraid to take an unpopular stand or to appropriately question group consensus • Readily takes appropriate measured risks
2 Proficient practitioner	• Demonstrates the confidence to direct others; readily assumes team leadership responsibility • Maintains own convictions in actions and decisions • Is willing to take an unpopular stand or question group consensus when necessary • Maintains own convictions in actions and decisions, yet indicates willingness to alter behavior based on valid suggestions of others • Can express forceful opinions, when necessary, without alienating others • Encourages team members to appropriately express their opinions and ideas • Helps build confidence among team members
1 Basic or elementary	• Is a self-assured self-starter; can take appropriate action without being overly dependent on the approval of others • Is willing to express opinions or assert ideas when required. Is willing to assert self to get own ideas heard • Has self-assurance in areas of core responsibility • Approaches new tasks with confidence • Accepts other opinions when appropriate
0 Inadequate	• Hesitant; seems tentative or unsure; may defer to others in order to win their approval • Readily acquiesces when challenged but seldom challenges others • Very dependent on the opinions of others; shows minimal self-confidence • Shows a reluctance to participate in meetings • Overly aggressive, too independent, stubborn, or inflexible

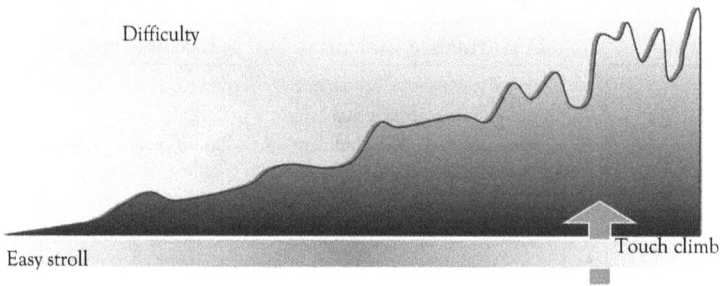

Figure 2.1 Assertiveness degree of difficulty

Best Ways to Develop This Competency

Continuous development to enhance strengths and remedy any liabilities is essential to maintaining self-esteem. Expertise, integrity, and communications, the three components of personal power, create confidence, which enables you to be assertive. These power sources can be used to build confidence.

Improving Your Capacity

> Those who undertake to develop their competence in *Assertiveness* should begin by developing a personal improvement plan. Start by inventorying your assets. You do have a lot to contribute, and knowing what that is can be a first step.
>
> Be aware of the importance of nonverbal communication when you express yourself. Up to 70 percent of what you communicate is nonverbal. Passive, weak body language can undermine what you are trying to say.
>
> READ: *When I Say No, I Feel Guilty*: for Managers and Executives, Volumes I and II by Manuel J. Smith. Bantam. 1975
>
> ATTEND: Many workshops are readily available on the topic. Most people find them very helpful.

Start Today

> Monitor your conversations for the next 24 hours. Note how many times you used *hedging* phrases: perhaps, possibly, if you don't mind, and so on. Avoid them in the future.

Pick a topic that you are knowledgeable and passionate about. Find an opportunity today to express yourself.

Consider times where you were assertive. What conditions enabled that behavior? How can you recreate those conditions?

Our three lenses for examining the competency *Assertiveness* once again illustrate the importance of emphasizing performance as the key definitional element, but also recognize the many other influences needed to build and evaluate required *Assertiveness*. This deeper understanding of each of the several dozen competencies found in most models is essential for effective applications. It is hard to assess, appraise, or develop competence without that deeper knowledge.

Questions for Reflection

1. Compare and contrast the three perspectives used in this chapter to examine the competency of *Assertiveness*. Which perspectives emphasize behavior and performance more?
2. What is meant by *mindset before skillset* in acquiring complex competence?
3. Evaluate your own current organizational role in terms of needed *Assertiveness*; where do you fall on the proficiency continuum?
4. Narrate an imaginary explanation, evaluation, and feedback session for someone who falls short in self-confidence.

CHAPTER 3

Competencies in the Context of Organizational Systems

In this chapter, we will reinforce the importance of using competencies as a shared language across applications in the context of an organization's business and talent management system. We will provide more background for how competencies impact an individual's career life cycle. We will also explore the most frequent competency applications and tools in organizational settings. We will theme these tools and applications across three broad areas: talent acquisition, talent development, and talent performance. We will also illustrate this career impact through an example of how a competency model is woven through the career of one organization's employee. Finally, we will explain how competency models can drive a high-performance culture in organizations.

Competencies as the Common Language Across Talent Management Systems

First, let us explain talent management as the method for how organizations align business objectives to plan, recruit, select, integrate, and develop people. Figure 3.1 captures the overall platform of a talent management system. Next, let us zoom out to address how competencies fit into an entire business system as the *complete* context for understanding their importance. Talent strategy begins with business strategy.[1] An organization's mission, core technology, and key differentiators all influence the knowledge, skill, and motivation needed in their employee populations. Clear understanding of the ideal employee derives from this starting point. Engineering organizations do hire engineers, but other key competencies such as *Customer Service Orientation* may differ dramatically between a manufacturing and a consulting engineering firm with intensely different purposes and business models.

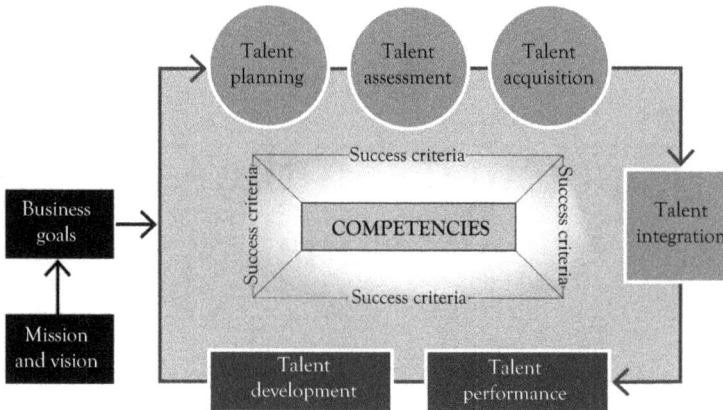

Figure 3.1 Talent management system driven by business needs

Business goals should inform every talent decision and provide the roadmap for what an organization wants to achieve with their products, services, and revenue goals. Organizations succeed or fail based on their talent.[2]

Living within these talent management systems, human resource professionals have often observed with interest, and with a little envy, that in many organizations the other primary staff functions of finance and information technology have successfully implemented universal systems with a common vocabulary and metrics, to optimize their effectiveness across the entire enterprise. In the specific case of finance, CFOs have realized that it is essential to implement standardized reporting systems and metrics to reliably measure and report relevant financial performance. One business unit cannot be measuring *net profit* while another measures earnings before interest, taxes, depreciation and amortization (EBITDA), or report return on net assets (RONA) versus return on invested capital (ROIC) and still present a coherent, consistent report of annual performance to stakeholders. Financial experts do admit that there are different terms and metrics that can effectively report revenue, profitability, and measures of economic value, *but* they also know that it is absolutely necessary to choose a standard set of terms and stick with it over time to optimize systems. Generally accepted accounting principles (GAAP) can provide standard terms, though within these guidelines custom variations can, and do, exist.

This same consistent approach should be a common practice in corporate human resources. But all too often, *different* criteria are used to hire, promote, evaluate, and train talent *within the same organization.* Recruiters will adopt one set of criteria, while succession managers use another, and trainers employ a third set as learning objectives. Of course, this leads to confusion on the part of line managers and inefficient (and probably ineffective) talent systems that should synergize across the enterprise. These conflicting models may actually *suboptimize* all of talent management. In one organization, we observed that one set of criteria was used in the hiring interviews for managers, a different set of behavioral standards was used in performance appraisal, and yet a third model for performance was employed in a 360° survey-guided development process. Of course, these conflicting standards caused confusion and tended to interfere with efficient and effective applications.

As has been reported in previous chapters, the easy remedy for this problem of conflicting criteria is to adopt a common set of valid criteria that can be reliably measured to support all talent systems across the enterprise. *Competency models* have become a recognized best practice to provide organizations with this consistent *blueprint* for ideal presentation.[3,4] Competency models can provide ideal criteria by which to compare candidates' skills with job needs in selection interviews or assessment centers. Or, taken from the same model, a subset of competencies can also help clarify individual role requirements and populate job descriptions, thus setting expectations to help in performance management. The same model can provide competencies as learning objectives in development programs, or as criteria in a 360°survey-guided leadership development experience. In this way, a common language is introduced to allow all talent management systems to talk to each other and reinforce organizational talent strategy.

Common Talent System Applications for Competency Models

Competencies are extremely useful in a broad range of applications across the organization. Having a common understanding of the elements of success provides the benchmark by which all the players know what is expected, and how well they are meeting the organization's needs. The major applications we will talk about here are:

1. Talent acquisition
2. Talent development
3. Talent performance
4. Competency, culture, and strategy.

Talent Acquisition

The most important decision an organization makes regarding its people is the decision to employ them. Every other decision is a consequence of this governing choice. In preparation for this important decision, the hiring manager can use competencies to establish position criteria. A common practice is using competencies to select the top six to eight that are representative of effective job performance. The use of competencies can create a productive discussion with position stakeholders regarding the framework for effective performance in a job. With criteria, talent acquisition can effectively identify and build candidate pools. Competency models provide the ideal template for comparing and contrasting candidates for a particular target role to facilitate this crucial decision. Assessing candidate readiness in terms of competence is most frequently accomplished through an interview, but other methods, such as assessment centers and online assessments, can also provide insight into an applicant's potential to perform.

Competency-Based Interviews

As mentioned, the most common *assessment* used globally to evaluate any candidate's readiness to assume a vacant organizational role is the interview. Research suggests that structuring an interview with a competency model (ideal criteria) and then using behavioral episode questioning can greatly increase interview efficacy.[5,6]

In this approach, a subset of valid competencies helps define job requirements and targeted questioning and then explores a candidate's performance background relevant to the competencies. For example, if *troubleshooting* is part of a customer service representative's job (and it usually is) then exploring the competency of *Problem Solving and Decision Making* in a candidate's history would help verify that capability. For instance, applicants for the customer service job might be asked to "describe a recent challenging problem with a customer you had to solve." This technique demands the interviewer to possess the skill to probe for details and surface enough specifics to establish sufficient narrative to assess future potential. Without this specific understanding, evaluation becomes a moving target and will vary from one person to the next. As a result, the interview process becomes more subjective and less accurate.

A variation in the standard sequential interview process is to conduct panel interviews composed of the hiring manager, human resources representative, and maybe other content experts, where specific behavioral questions are asked and all panel members hear the responses and independently judge the candidates' readiness. While seemingly more cumbersome, panel interviews actually can be more efficient than the sequential (and seemingly endless) interviews that are often used.

To help organize the execution of a panel interview, a planning tool should be prepared in advance to determine where each interviewer will focus (see Table 3.1). For example, after first identifying the competencies to be assessed, the interview team develops behavioral episode interview questions for each relevant competency area, along with follow-up questions to probe further and help the candidate to elaborate. Finally, the questions are distributed among the interviewers to ensure that all competencies are covered and none are redundant.

Assessment Centers

Assessment centers are really a process, not a place, and have been a best practice talent diagnostic technique since the 1950s. The process is best described by the *Standards and Ethics for Assessment Center Operations.* The standards formally define an assessment center as a process that "consists of a standardized evaluation of behavior based on numerous inputs. Multiple trained observers and techniques are used. Judgments about behavior are made, in part, from specifically developed assessment simulations."[7] While there are variations on this theme, the basic elements of an assessment center have all stood the test of time and have provided

Table 3.1 Panel interview planning tool

	Competency 1 *Assertiveness*	Competency 2 Communication skills	Competency 3 *Initiative*
Interviewer A	Q1: Describe a time you had to be assertive in order to complete an important project or work task …	Q2: What has been your …	Q3: Can you think of a situation in which you …
	Follow-up:	*Follow-up:*	*Follow-up:*
Interviewer B	Q1: Can you share an experience in championing your ideas when they may have been unpopular …	Q2: Have you ever been involved in …	Q3: Have you ever found yourself in a position …
	Follow-up:	*Follow-up:*	*Follow-up:*
Interviewer C	Q1: Can you tell us about a time when you might have come on too strong, or maybe overstepped yourself …	Q2: Can you describe a difficult situation in which you had to …	Q3: Have you ever had to …
	Follow-up:	*Follow-up:*	*Follow-up:*

dozens of criteria-related validity studies proving the efficacy of the process. These required elements are:

1. A valid competency model providing evaluation criteria.
2. A set of exercises simulating professional life in an organization, exercises might include:
   a. Leaderless group discussions
   b. In-basket simulations
   c. Business case analyses and presentations
   d. Role-plays
3. Three or more trained assessors who triangulate on participant scoring.
4. A rigorous assessment methodology.

Centers are often used to inform organizational selection decisions, especially when the target role is the first-line supervisor. When many in the applicant pool are individual contributors, and have not performed in the target role, assessments and measures based on job history are less predictive. For example, if a sales manager suddenly resigns, the organization naturally looks to the sales representatives reporting to the now vacant role for possible replacements. Of course, the two roles have dramatically different skill sets and choosing the best sales person, without testing their leadership and management motivation and competence, can often end badly. In the worst case, the organization loses an excellent seller and gains a mediocre manager who soon derails. Assessment centers can help make a better selection decision by testing candidates in the competencies they will have to possess, and situations they will have to face, as a *manager* and not as an individual contributor.

Online Assessments

While there are too many to be detailed here, it should be noted that another option for evaluating competency readiness is through the myriad paper and pencil (written) examinations available. These can be delivered in proctored settings or online. Literally thousands of tests are now available to measure the social and cognitive aspects of competence. For example, any number of tests can measure the intelligence factor of a competency such as *Learning Agility* or *Problem Solving*. Other tests measure underlying natural influences on emotional intelligence such as agreeableness, conscientiousness, or extroversion, which show up in competencies such as *Relationship Building* and *Sensitivity*.

Finally, it should be noted that, in the context of selection, competency models used for hiring also help ensure good person-job *fit* and thus increase the likelihood of retention. Good orientation helps to set the stage for retention, but a strong competency evaluation in the selection process also translates into hiring managers who are able to work closely with the new hires to reinforce positive competency behaviors and shore up any deficits.

Talent Development

The heart and soul of successful and sustainable organizational performance comes from the continuous development of a capable workforce.

Initial orientation and training followed by ongoing development are essential to staying relevant in today's ever-changing world. Competencies provide a necessary framework for these ongoing learning and development efforts.

The American Society of Training and Development notes that developing (training) an employee without any diagnosis is like planting cut flowers! And, likewise, in the health care world, if you prescribe without diagnosing you may be guilty of malpractice. You need to diagnose, or *prepare the soil* first to determine readiness and more precisely target the training. Consequently many competency-based learning applications involve individual assessment as the first step in a developmental cycle.

Orientation and Integration

Though often neglected, initial talent integration, or *onboarding*, is a golden opportunity to discuss role clarity and explain the requirements for effective performance to a new employee, including the competencies essential for effective performance. The moment new people enter the organization or start a new job, they are eager to assimilate and perform as quickly as possible. As an organization, you never get a second chance for this first impression. One study demonstrated that 86 percent of new hires decided to stay or leave the organization *within their first six months*.[8] Organizations create a competitive advantage when they integrate their talent quickly and set competency and learning expectations in advance.

Competency-Based Survey-Guided Development—360° Surveys

Increasingly popular in recent years has been the use of a competency model as the diagnostic template for a survey-guided development effort. These multirater surveys, popularly called 360°s, have become a best-practice leadership development tool now used in the majority of large American organizations. These surveys are called 360°s because a participating manager asks for feedback from all points on the compass surrounding him or her on an organization chart: their boss (to the north), their peers (to the east and to the west), and direct reports (to the south).

The typical 360° survey includes the following elements:

- Participants identify and invite anonymous feedback on their competence from organizational peers and direct reports. Identified raters are limited to those who have known the participant long enough to reliably rate them. Bosses are included, but are not promised anonymity. Once respondents are selected, typically a third party administers an online survey to those identified. Most 360°s solicit feedback from a dozen or more respondents.
- The surveys employ rating scales to judge and compare perceived proficiency across relevant competencies by the different respondent groups. These quantitative results allow normative comparisons. More robust surveys also solicit open-ended written comments to ensure more complete and specific feedback.
- To ensure that participants understand, own, and act on the survey results, they are packaged into a feedback report and a qualified coach delivers the feedback and helps interpret the report for them.
- Accountability for any needed improvement surfaced by the survey is ensured through a variety of options, including ongoing coaching, developmental objectives required in performance appraisal documents, follow-up surveys, and informal continuing feedback.
- Typically, repeat surveys occur a year or two after the initial survey. Occasionally *pulse* surveys are administered more quickly and target the specific subset of competencies the participant may be trying to improve.
- Because of issues with politicizing the process and rater accuracy, the vast majority of 360°s are used strictly for development. While it is tempting to use 360° feedback for administrative purposes (e.g., informing annual appraisal ratings or succession management readiness evaluations), experience has shown that these applications can damage the 360° reputation and introduce negative power and political dynamics into the process.

Many organizations have used 360° leadership development processes for years and managers have been through several cycles allowing measurement of progress on targeted areas.

Competencies as Learning Objectives in Workshops

Once an organization has a valid competency model in place, individual competencies that are common to a given role or band (e.g., entry-level supervisor) easily translate into learning objectives. For example, many entry-level supervisory training programs, whether online or in classroom settings, teach basic competencies such as *Active Listening*, *Problem Solving*, *Organizing and Planning* (*Time Management*), and *Communications*. These workshops use a variety of instructional techniques including lecture, case study, exercises, and simulations.

Sometimes an individual competency, such as *Presentation Skills*, becomes the single learning focus for a workshop. In a typical two-day workshop, participants may experience a lecture on the elements of the ideal public speech (i.e., clear purpose and use of stories, facts, quotes to build credibility, obvious animation and enthusiasm, plus instruction in the use of multiple media, etc.). Then trainees might observe (via video) good and bad speeches to compare and contrast techniques. And finally, the majority of time in learning this skill-based competency would probably be spent on delivering speeches and receiving feedback. Practice, practice, practice!

Other more cognitive competencies, such as *Financial Acumen*, lend themselves as learning objectives for online training. There are a number of very good web-based programs that clearly present the basics of finance (i.e., how to read income statements, balance sheets, cash flows, economic valuations, etc.) and then use exercises such annual report analysis to consolidate the learning and test the learner.

Competencies for Career Planning and Mentoring

Once again, if an organization has a valid, and comprehensive, competency model it automatically provides clear criteria for employee career planning. Coupled with interest, value, and motivational assessments, the advertised required competence for a target role can help individuals investigate and make future career choices.

While many managers attribute personal development to informal mentors and coaches, many organizations have installed formal mentor programs to enhance career planning and succession management efforts. Often coupled with the 360° process outlined above, a mentor matched to an appropriate protégé provides feedback, coaching, and counseling. One technique for matching mentors and protégés is to couple a potential competency weakness with a mentor's strength for targeted coaching. Another approach is to couple assessment center diagnosis with mentor programs to provide an initial diagnosis to help shape the coaching agenda.

Competency Coaching

Under the learning and development umbrella the widespread use of internal and external management coaches has come of age in recent years. Organizations such as The Hudson Institute and International Coaching Federation provide certification programs to ensure proper training and experience. In a typical engagement, the certified coach is retained by an organization and then initiates a diagnosis (e.g., 360° survey plus personality assessment) and begins a development cycle of feedback, action planning, implementation, and follow-up.

Competencies in Talent Performance

Talent performance also known as performance management refers to the process of communicating specific position expectations, and then managing an individual's performance against those expectations. In point of fact, individuals can manage their own performance efforts when they clearly and comprehensively know what is expected of them.[9] While providing the needed role clarity at the outset seems to be rudimentary, many organizations do not take the time needed.

Competencies help define expected behavior in jobs and organizations. These behaviors can and should be part of defining performance as a way to link it to the right outcomes. Figure 3.2 illustrates a typical performance management cycle from setting business goals and specifying

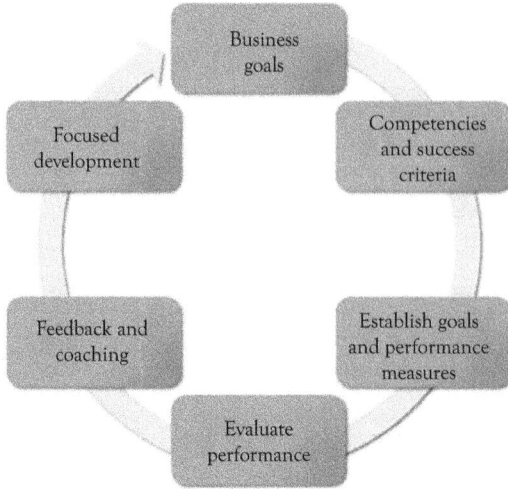

Figure 3.2 Performance management cycle

required competence to establishing and monitoring individual performance supplemented with feedback and coaching.

The use of competency models in the performance management
process also switches the focus from *what* employees do, to *how* they
do it. This realignment reflects an overall move to a developmental
approach to performance management. The use of competency models
in the appraisal process results in "more qualitative, longer range, future-
oriented information which is used for employee development and career
path planning."[10]

The following is a list of organizational issues that indicate a need for
competency-based performance management:[11]

- Job performance standards and appraisal criteria are seen as
  unfair.
- Performance appraisals are not taken seriously because they
  have little impact on employee performance or development.
- The performance management system does not reflect or
  reinforce the organization's strategy because it fails to focus
  employee behavior on strategic priorities such as quality or
  service.
- Performance ratings are inflated.

In the context of coaching during performance management, competencies also allow managers to redirect marginal employee performance more objectively by providing a template for diagnosing *why* the desired objectives or standards have been missed. For example, one of the first places to look into when helping a new supervisor who misses deadlines or milestones may be the competency *Delegation*. Are they trying to do all the work themselves? Are they micromanaging? Have they learned to release appropriate authority to fully use all their team members? Once diagnosed, competencies can then provide a clear developmental path forward in terms of acquiring needed knowledge and skill.

A competency-based appraisal can also make explicit the different levels of proficiency required *within* a specific competency. A good competency model will use a measurement scale to differentiate the levels of competence, thus helping to differentiate between effective and noneffective performance. For example, if an employee scores low on competency measurement, the actual, and required, behaviors are readily available. With a scale, it is easy to start a conversation regarding the specific levels of proficiency needed for acceptable performance.

In sum, it can be seen that identifying clear competency requirements for jobs, levels, or functions can allow organizations to pivot and apply the same competencies to position descriptions, hiring and succession criteria, as well as learning objectives for development programs such as mentoring, training, or survey-guided development. Once again it is competencies that knit these common applications together and integrate them.

Competencies and Strategy: Building Models to Drive a High-Performance Culture

Competency models have an automatic head start over other job analytic techniques in reinforcing organizational goals and building a high-performance organization, as they typically derive from research on *high performers* in a specific organizational context. Best practice modeling techniques employ interviews and investigations into the competencies it takes to consistently produce positive results across a balanced score card (i.e., key metrics of success in finance, talent, operations, and customer/consumer).

One set of popular criteria for isolating high performers for emulation[12] includes these four filters:

1. *Results*: Model individuals who have produced tangible, relevant, and persistent results in their function and at their level.
2. *Respect*: Model individuals who have generated a positive reputation of trust and accomplishment.
3. *Passion*: Model individuals who clearly enjoy their roles and working in a specific context (industry, organization, role).
4. *Likeability*: Model individuals with team skills; those who work well with others.

When models are built to emulate internal high performers with these characteristics, and concomitant track records, and when the models are used to hire, promote, appraise, and develop internal talent, they *automatically* support a high-performance organization.

Indeed the modeling process itself can be seen as an organization development (OD) intervention to help build or reinforce a high-performance culture. Most good modeling projects follow a classic OD approach[13] in development in that they:

1. Employ behavioral science theory and application
2. Are driven from the top down across *all* the organization
3. Invite involvement (and hence commitment)
4. Provide a feedback and adjustment loop (action learning)
5. Prepare the organization to manage change

Culture building typically takes years, and a common competency model that inflects strategic priorities and is applied in *every* talent management system can provide a culture change catalyst and constant reinforcement.

For example, a large consumer sports apparel supplier modified a commercially available model to reinforce their strategic emphasis on aggressive growth—a brand with personality, innovative design, and global reach. The model provided a consistent dictionary of relevant competencies that were used in recruiting, competency-based interviewing, assessment centers, performance management, and as criteria in leadership development programs and 360° survey-guided development programs. The competency model reinforced a consumer focused, creative, and growth-oriented matrix organization and ensured that the right talent was hired, promoted, appraised, and trained to support that culture.

Competency models ensure that the right development activities are in alignment with organizational strategy. As discussed earlier, aligning competencies with organizational strategy provides the right direction for the talent management system. With this in mind, focusing on the right training and development initiatives that support the organizational strategy ensures that the time and resources devoted will be well utilized. Using a competency model helps remove doubt on where to focus limited resources toward developing people.

Putting It All Together: One Employee's Competency Journey

Figure 3.3 illustrates how a common model can integrate talent management in a typical career life cycle. From the first hiring interview as a candidate for an individual contributor role, to the final panel interview for a strategic leadership position 20 years later, a competency model informed individual and organizational choices. The journey also includes into the context the common applications described previously.

To illustrate this career path, and to emphasize how central a standard competency model is to an integrated talent management system, one professional's story in a well-managed organization might go like this:

*Meet Piper Chatman. She graduated with a business degree, with an emphasis in finance, from a well-known California university and entered the job market. She attended interviews in a number of accounting firms and larger technology companies in the San Francisco Bay area. She received several offers, but really liked a technology company named Hi-Teck. In particular, she was impressed with their professional **interview process**, as the questions were relevant, both to her experience and to the advertised role (financial analyst), and she felt she was afforded the opportunity to demonstrate her competence. She accepted Hi-Teck's offer, and after hiring found out that during the interview she was being compared to the company's competency model of an ideal analyst, with questions designed to explore her performance*

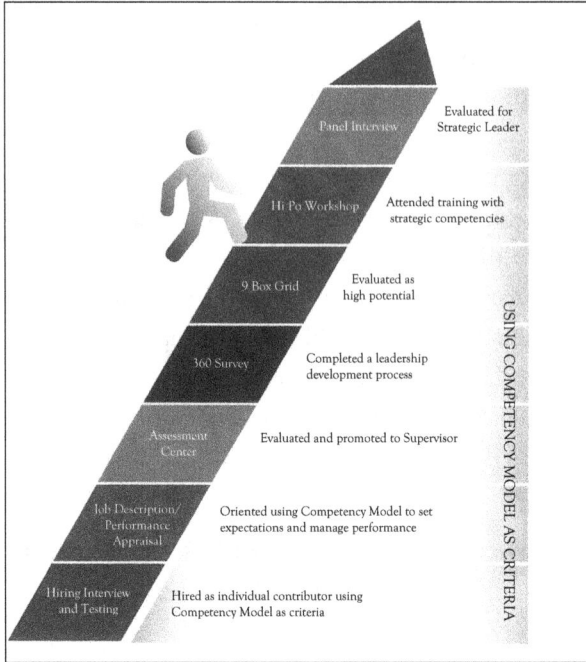

Figure 3.3 Competencies in 20-year career trajectory

background relevant to the knowledge, skill, and motivation necessary for exceptional performance in the target role. This was Piper's first exposure to Hi-Teck's competency model.

*During her orientation to the company, Piper's HR representative presented a **job model** to further clarify her role and set expectations. In addition to standard information on her responsibilities, the position description also listed eight competencies essential to her success at Hi-Teck. These included Financial Acumen (her core skill set), and other competencies like Team Skills, Problem Solving and Decision Making, and Communications. The interview had confirmed Piper's necessary proficiency in all these competencies and made explicit the areas in which she needed to stay current.*

*Within a few weeks of arriving, Piper's manager met with her to discuss Hi-Teck's annual **performance management** process. Piper was being assigned to support Hi-Teck's retail operation, and her primary business goals involved milestones and deadlines for the roll-out of a new financial results tracking system. The performance management system also included personal growth goals, as Hi-Teck wanted to set the expectation with every associate* *that continuous personal growth was an imperative. While Piper was judged to be proficient in the competencies necessary for her role, she expressed an additional goal to acquire more Industry Knowledge in Hi-Teck's business in order to gain more credibility and contextual understanding of how the finance function could better partner with its business customers. Progress toward goal accomplishment in this competency was an essential part of Piper's annual review.*

An integral part of Hi-Teck's **succession management** *process was to use a Promotion Readiness Index (PRI) to measure both potential and performance. The PRI was based on competencies required at the next level in the talent pipeline in order to seed each function with potential leaders. Piper's initial employment interview had revealed not only the technical expertise she needed to hit the ground running, but also the potential to move into supervisory roles later in her career. Piper had held several leadership roles in her university and also demonstrated exceptional Informal Communications and Relationship Building competence, all of which were needed in supervisory roles.*

During the next few years, Piper's manager used the **annual performance appraisal** *meeting to test her interest in advancing into a supervisory role someday. Piper also took an online* **career planning workshop** *that asked her to explore her interest and aptitude in the competencies necessary for supervision. She liked responsibility and working with people, and received positive feedback regarding her choice to move into management.*

After five years of successful performance at Hi-Teck, Piper had moved from her entry-level role to a senior analyst position with excellent internal customer feedback, and stellar performance reviews. Piper had learned from her HR representative and her manager that twice a year Hi-Teck offered high-potential associates the chance to test their readiness in the competencies necessary to move up the career ladder into supervision at an **assessment center***. The assessment center employed simulations such as group discussions, role-plays, in-basket exercises, and business case presentations to test candidate readiness to be promoted to supervision. Trained internal managers observed Piper's performance in the simulations and evaluated her readiness to assume a supervisory role in competencies such as Organizing and Planning, Delegation, Communications, Influence, Relationship Building, and Problem Solving. The assessment center revealed that Piper did indeed* *have the potential to move into supervision, and she was put into the pool for consideration for the next opening for a supervisory position in finance or a related function.*

*Within six months of completing evaluation at the assessment center Piper was promoted to Accounting Supervisor. For the next few years, she continued to advance and maintained an excellent **performance management** record. She also joined Hi-Teck's **mentoring program** to help young professionals successfully assimilate into the company's culture, and explore their own growth potential. She developed an excellent reputation as a coach and had a track record of selecting and developing exceptional talent for Hi-Teck. During her years as a manager, Piper participated three times in Hi-Teck's **360° survey-guided development process**. In this process, she received feedback against Hi-Teck's competency model from her boss, self, peers, and direct reports. The process was strictly developmental, with Piper having the option of using survey feedback to drive her annual development goal. Piper took her feedback to heart, and learned to better leverage her strengths while she addressed developmental opportunities, both formally and informally.*

*Aided by regular feedback, Piper moved up the managerial ladder and continued to grow and excel as a leader. Hi-Teck's annual **succession management** process was also tasked with recommending individuals for participation in the company's strategic leadership development program. The company had long recognized that being a good functional manager did not necessarily qualify you to move to the C suite, where strategy and vision were the key differentiators. The program to take good functional leaders and develop them to be strategic leaders was anchored by a **leadership development workshop using a simulation** to teach strategic competencies such as Visioning, Business Systems Thinking, Strategic Thinking, and Financial Acumen in an enterprise context. Following her successful completion of the workshop, Piper volunteered to serve on an **action learning team** that had been assigned a strategic problem to solve for the company. These teams not only provided valuable input to Hi-Teck's senior leaders, but also included peer feedback to continue to develop as potential strategic leaders.*

*One day the chief financial officer announced his retirement after 20 years with the company, and Piper applied for the role. The selection process for any direct report of the CEO required a **panel interview** with all six members of the senior leadership team. This interview employed questioning techniques similar to Piper's initial interview many years ago, but of course now she had to* *demonstrate a performance history that would qualify her for a strategic role—that of a CFO. The interview questions were centered on the competencies of Strategic Thinking, Team Management, Visioning, and Business Systems.*

Piper was selected as the company's new CFO. While thanking her senior leaders for their confidence, she attributed a good share of her success to the clear expectations and developmental support provided by Hi-Teck's competency model. It had provided a needed blueprint, with reliable and valid feedback techniques along the way, which had accelerated her growth and revealed her potential. A final confidence boosting conclusion for Piper looking back on her career was a realization that by applying a transparent competency based approach, her company had assured that she was ready for the current promotion and knew what to do to prepare for the next one. Politics and preference were minimized and she felt good she had earned her position in the C suite.

Benefits of a Competency-Based Talent Management System

Business needs must drive talent needs. Failure to connect the two will result in different talent agendas across the organization. Good competency modeling provides a fundamental building block in talent management to produce the employee behavior to drive needed business results. Table 3.2 summarizes the advantages of building and applying a valid model.

Table 3.2 Benefits of competency models in talent management systems

Talent management system element	Core competency benefits
Talent assessment	• Informs the required success criteria for talent management systems • Provides direction for using validated assessment
Talent acquisition	• Provides a clear framework for the interview process • Informs good talent selection
Talent integration	• Clarifies the competencies required for the role • Increases the likelihood of retention
Talent performance	• Helps define the measurement for job success • Provides a shared understanding of what is expected
Talent development	• Provides focus on areas for talent development • Ensures that the right development activities are in alignment with organizational strategy

Competencies not only integrate complete organization wide talent management systems but also help individuals link together all the tools needed for job performance and career management. Experience has shown that employing a common language of competence can optimize talent assessment, acquisition, and integration. Using competencies on the front end of the talent management system will ensure benefits in their later use for talent appraisal and talent development.

Competencies and the Link to Diversity

The business case for a diverse workforce has been well established. Propelled by not only legal requirements for objective hiring practices but also a growing body of evidence suggesting the benefits of a diverse work-place, and by the correlation between an organization's financial success and the greater innovation provided by a diverse, and divergent, employee population.[14] These benefits are the direct outcome of acquiring diverse talent.

Diversity and competencies (e.g., job success criteria) go hand in hand during talent acquisition. Competencies provide a strong, objective foundation for an unbiased recruitment and selection process. Competencies are blind to race, gender, religion, or sexual orientation. Instead, they provide the structure to fight bias and ensure fair treatment. To succeed, it is important to create and implement specific talent acquisition practices that will help drive desired diversity hiring outcomes (See Table 3.3).[15]

Table 3.3 Practices for diverse talent acquisition

Practices	Outcomes
Developing a diversity talent acquisition strategy in alignment with organizational areas in need of diverse talent	Builds a targeted diverse talent pool aligned with organizational goals
Developing success profiles (e.g., job descriptions) anchored in job related competencies	Provides clear criteria and outcomes for success in specific roles
Establishing a structured selection process based on relevant competencies	Increases the probability of hiring the best candidates
Developing onboarding strategies	Outlines the path for success in the role of and integration into organizational culture

Integrating competencies into a talent acquisition process offers the necessary objectivity to help provide a fair process for a competent, diverse candidate pool. Competencies also provide support by informing the onboarding of new hires through role clarity and a coaching structure.[16] These practices ultimately help pick the best, most diverse talent.

Questions for Reflection

1. Provide three examples of competency applications in specific talent management systems for hiring, promotion, appraisal, or training.
2. Discuss at least four incidences when an employee might encounter competencies in a 20-year career arc.
3. How are competencies used in onboarding and appraising employees?
4. Discuss how competency modeling can be considered an organizational development effort.
5. Discuss how competencies add value across diverse applications such as assessment centers or employee orientation programs.
6. Discuss the key elements that define a classic assessment center.
7. What competencies might form the learning objectives for an entry level supervisor workshop?
8. How can competencies help in diagnosing and developing a poor performer?
9. What is survey-guided leadership development?
10. How does your talent strategy align with your business goals and objectives? What can be done to ensure better alignment?
11. How do organizations create an environment to attract, recruit, develop, reward, and retain the right people?

CHAPTER 4

Universal Competencies: The *Big Six* (Plus One)

In this chapter, we will expand on our previous reference to a set of competencies shared across a wide range of roles and organizations. Research shows that six competencies consistently rise to the top of any competency model.[1] These six competencies can truly help differentiate high performers and can also provide a foundation for understanding universal job requirements. Using these competencies as a framework to judge and develop talent can be a powerful tool in ensuring that the best employees populate your organization. We will thoroughly explore each of these competencies and offer ideas for identifying and developing them. We will close with a reference to a seventh competency entitled *Functional* and *Technical* expertise, which recognizes the additional importance of specific job content within the mix of required competence.

Along those lines it is important to note that these *Big Six* assume that an employee already possesses the necessary technical and industry expertise (e.g., a financial analyst has an MBA in finance). In point of fact, these *hard* technical skills are relatively easy to assess and validate; but it is the *soft* skills represented in the Big Six that can really differentiate *exceptional* performance, especially in leadership roles. In fact, it is an axiom among human resources professionals that we tend to hire for the hard skills but fire for the soft skills.

Here are the Big Six:

1. *Relationship Building and Sensitivity* (emotional intelligence)
2. *Problem Solving and Decision Making* (creative analysis and good judgment)
3. *Influence* (accumulation and skillful use of power)
4. *Drive and Energy* (passion to perform)

5. *Organizing and Planning* (being efficient and focusing energy and resources on the right thing)
6. *Communications Cluster* (clear, frequent information in the right medium)

Let us explore each one in detail.

Relationship Building – It Is All About Relationships!

At a professional conference in Chicago one of the featured speakers was the leadership guru Dr. Warren Bennis, who was a distinguished professor of business administration at the University of Southern California in Los Angeles. The late Dr. Bennis, once considered the world's leading expert on leadership, began his talk by noting that in his six decades of studying the topic, he could draw just two unassailable conclusions. The entire audience shifted to the edge of their seats, pens in hand, to record what he had to say:

"First, leadership makes a tremendous difference."

Isn't this obvious? Not necessarily, if you judge the process by which organizations often haphazardly select and develop leaders. Tom Peters, the noted speaker and coauthor of the classic *In Search of Excellence*, said it best: "A good leader doesn't just marginally improve a team's performance; a good leader can add an order of magnitude to a team's results". All too often, organizations—and leaders themselves—dramatically underestimate the impact that leadership, good or bad, makes.

"Second, leadership is about relationships."

This also seems to be obvious but again requires insight. Too often, leadership is presented as an intellectual exercise, with managers told to analyze a situation and then react with a scripted set of behaviors. But effective leaders are able to connect with their followers on an emotional level that comes more from the heart than the head—their EQ, or emotional intelligence, as contrasted to their IQ.[2]

EQ is a harder concept to nail down than IQ. While there is no single number or measure that wraps it up neatly, exceptional leaders with a high level of emotional intelligence do have common attributes:[3]

- They understand that nurturing productive relationships is a primary driver for their success.
- They like interacting with people and are good at it.
- They devote appropriate time and energy to establishing and maintaining networks.
- They value and respect the concerns of others, and this compassion translates into behaviors that communicate empathy toward others, respect for the individual, and appreciation of diversity among team members.
- They initiate contacts readily and maintain them over time. They leverage these relationships to facilitate business transactions.

Can you improve your EQ? Our experience has shown that managers believe that acquiring skill and knowledge in *Relationship Building and Sensitivity* can be daunting (especially if you are naturally disposed against it)—and with a good reason. This is a competency that should definitely be on a list of required criteria when you select a team member, as it is so challenging to develop after the fact.

To ensure that a candidate qualifies for a role, look for trends in his or her history that indicate a preference for teams and community. If you are using the best practice technique of behavioral episode interviewing (i.e., asking candidates to describe specific situations in which they have been successful or unsuccessful with interpersonal relations), use the interview to explore situations in which they have been in conflict with others or had to deliver bad news. These critical incidents can reveal comfort and competence in difficult situations.

If you are trying to develop this competency in yourself, remember the saying *mind-set before skill set*. That is, your disposition and ingrained attitudes can be more important than skills that can be learned. You will need to reflect on your thoughts and feelings about others. For instance, what motivates you in interpersonal situations? If you tend to distrust people, then ask why? There are many reasons to value relationships and build genuine connections with others, including the need for a social network during stress or crisis, or the importance of being genuine in sensitive interpersonal situations. But you will have to find your own inspiration to drive your development.

There have been many studies about why people fail in organizations.[4] Most of them identified broken trust and political incompetence as primary factors. Once again, this failure has to do with an inability to understand others and build solid, open, and genuine relationships.

Too often, organizations select frontline leaders based on technical expertise (and more and more frontline jobs require a *working supervisor* who has that knowledge), but then the management succession pool becomes seeded with *technocrats* who ascend to higher, and more powerful, leadership roles. Here, their lack of EQ is exposed and their careers go off track.

Problem Solving and Decision Making: Decisions, Decisions!

As an exercise in minimalism, the authors were once asked by a client to select, from a list of several dozens, the two most important leadership competencies for good management. The choice was easy: *Influence*, or your personal power to persuade, and *Problem Solving and Decision Making*, which can define you as a leader through your legacy of decisions.

Research and experience tell us that these two competencies are among those that have the biggest impact on an organization. Making good decisions and solving thorny problems involves knowing about and executing a systematic process. From the simple *ready, aim, fire* model (or *ready, fire, aim* practiced by many *former* executives), to more complicated models involving root cause analysis, creative thinking, risk analysis of options, and project management follow-through, all involve a certain defined progression. Understanding this implicit structure is fundamental to being an exceptional decision maker. The overall process of making good decisions requires proficiency in two potentially contradictory arenas: divergent thinking (thinking sideways) and convergent thinking (being decisive).[5]

Divergent or creative capability is required when initially confronting a decision. It is at this point that assumptions and paradigms (stereotypical or preset ways of thinking) can blind a decision maker to better options. For example, if the problem is *excessive turnover in the call center*, there may be a tendency to jump to the first solution that comes to mind (e.g., we need a better selection process).

However, a better starting point would be to hit the mental *pause* button and examine the root cause of the turnover. Research suggests that six factors influence retention: pay equity, benefits equity, good working conditions, quality supervision, opportunity to advance or grow, and the work itself.[6] Exploring all of these possible contributing factors would probably lead to a better solution.

Once root cause analysis and a creative exploration of options are complete, it is time for convergent thinking—pulling the decision trigger. This involves some risk-taking. In a word, you must be decisive; then, you must be ready to sell and defend your decision as needed. Roger Von Oech, one of Silicon Valley's most famous creativity consultants, characterizes the decision-making process in terms of four characters, or personalities, that you must be able to adopt. In the divergent phase, you must be an explorer and an artist, while in the convergent phase, you must be a judge and a warrior.[7]

When making decisions, personality also can come into play, potentially helping or hindering the process. You may have a natural disposition to act quickly—and perhaps prematurely. Or, you may be very creative in generating information and options but hesitant to pull the trigger. The Myers–Briggs type indicator, a widely used personality assessment tool, can provide insight into your decision-making preferences.[8] We recommend that all managers take the inventory early in their careers to get a better insight into their own preferences.

And what role does intuition play? When should you trust your gut? In his book *Blink*, Malcolm Gladwell notes that while intuition provides lightning-fast insight into a problem, it is most reliable after years of experience in a specific decision-making context.[9] Vic Braden, the famous tennis pro, could nearly unerringly predict if a player would *fault* on a serve in the milliseconds after a ball was tossed in the air. But it was his years of playing and coaching in the world of pro tennis that guided his insight. Though intuition plays a part, be careful when extrapolating your intuitive insight from one context to a less familiar one.

So what does all this tell us about learning to be a better decision maker or selecting leaders who can fill those roles? The decision-making process can be broken down and understood, which means that it can also be learned. Also, because the *Problem Solving and Decision Making* competency is so important to a manager's success, it should be part of any hiring or promotion decision. Asking candidates to describe their best or worst decisions, or using an in-basket exercise to test their problem solving ability during the interview, can help screen for this most important competency.

Influence: The Skillful Use of Power

As a manager, ask yourself honestly: Do your people do what you ask because they respect you, or because they respect the position you hold? This is not an academic question, mind you—employees will follow orders because the chain of command confers authority, and because they seek the rewards that come with compliance. But truly engaged employees—your best performers—are more productive when they are motivated to perform out of respect for you as a person and a leader.[10]

Your ability to influence, or your personal power to persuade, is one of two primary competencies that define successful leadership (the other is *Problem Solving and Decision Making*, which we discussed earlier). *Influence* is the focal competency for understanding how to persuade others and gain commitment. It identifies the special set of behaviors and motivations that leaders need to attract others to their agenda and to motivate them to act on their goals.

Situational Leadership

Experts tend to approach the *Influence* competency from two very different directions. The more widely adopted approach has been situational, in which leaders alternate between a more directive style to a more collaborative style depending on the circumstance. For example, an intern fresh from school would need more guidance and specific instructions at first—a directive style. As the beginner gains knowledge, skill, and confidence, the leader would shift to a more collaborative and participative approach. Ultimately the leader would be able to delegate responsibilities to a fully competent team member with broad guidance and minimal supervision.

In special circumstances, a more authoritarian style may be necessary, such as those involving a safety or integrity violation in which the consequences are severe. In such instances, leaders need to act swiftly and assertively to confront and correct the situation. Conversely, in special counseling circumstances during which dictating an outcome would be inappropriate, leaders need to be more participative. This approach may apply when offering career or life advice.

Sources of Power

The second approach to leadership, which we believe is more instructive in defining a true leader, identifies the sources of power that authorize leaders. These power sources can be presented on a continuum arranged from positional (granted by an organization) to personal (a portable form of authority granted by followers to an individual). Figure 4.1 illustrates this concept.[11] At one end are all the fixed positional power sources of role, reward (authority to pay, promote, and so on), and discipline (authority to punish) to the portable power sources of integrity (respect and reputation through being fair, honest, and open), expertise, and communications.

As anyone in an official supervisory position has been delegated authority to reward or punish their direct reports, the role itself grants an aura of power that allows the supervisor to direct others. These sources are fundamentally transactional in nature. For example, if an employee conforms to assigned duties and standards, the reward is keeping the job,

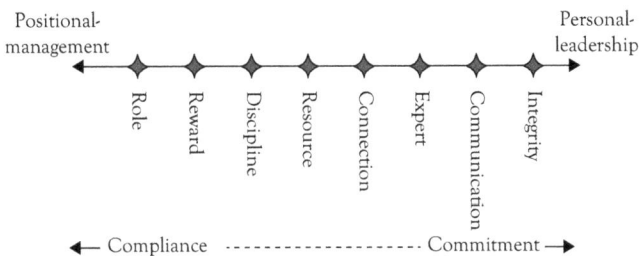

Figure 4.1 The power continuum

receiving a bonus, or earning time off. Those who do not comply face discipline. While this performance *contract* might gain compliance, it does not ensure commitment.

True leadership is found at the other end of the power continuum. If you think of the best leaders you have encountered—those who produce exceptional results, and who are widely respected, generally likeable, and passionate about what they do—you've probably noticed that they operate out of a personal power base. They are honest, open, and fair experts who are excellent communicators of a legitimate agenda. They generate personal power from three sources: expertise, skillful communications, and integrity, and are often sought out for advice. You grant them power by permitting them to influence you because of who they are.

In daily life, we often encounter examples of 'expert' leadership, or people whom we acknowledge that they know more about a subject than we do. The power that comes from being a great communicator is a little more complex. Martin Luther King's "I have a dream" speech is a case of 12 minutes of elegant oratory that moved a nation. But being a great public speaker is not a prerequisite to being a powerful communicator. To be one, you must first perfect your message, or what you intend to communicate. And keep in mind that grooming, dress, gestures, and inflection matter. In his book *Silent Messages*, Albert Mehrabian, professor emeritus of psychology at the University of California, Los Angeles, estimates that about 70 percent of the impact of every message is nonverbal.[12] For leaders, the entire world is a stage, and they must perfect and carefully transmit their intended message.

Much of the *Influence* competency can be learned, but there is an important element that needs to be confirmed before promoting someone into a leadership role. We call this quality *leadership identity*, or having the natural inclination and motivation to assume responsibility over others. The famous Harvard researcher David McClelland noted that anyone who wants to lead requires a *need for power* motivation.[13] Edgar Schein from MIT calls this characteristic *general management competence*.[14] Because some candidates for leadership roles may be motivated just by ambition, or the dark side of power, organizations need to ensure that candidates will truly resonate in leadership roles before promoting them.

Drive and Energy: Driven to Succeed, but by What?

Next, we will tackle an extremely important competency: *Drive and Energy.* This competency is absolutely essential for any employee yet it is difficult—if not impossible—to acquire through training. In fact, this attribute is usually present inherently within the individual (or not). Drive and energy are manifested in the passion and stamina that extraordinary professionals demonstrate on a daily basis.

What Drives Your High Performers?

A person's motivation is an extremely complex matter, and there are multiple theories on the topic. Abraham Maslow, the famous psychologist, theorized a human motivational need hierarchy composed of a series of satisfaction thresholds; each threshold is a necessary, but not sufficient, requirement for ascending to a more mature motivational state.[15] The first threshold is existential (i.e., the basic needs for food, water, shelter, safety, and so on); the next is the tribal motivation to have satisfactory relationships. Only when those needs are met can one finally rise to pure growth and actualization motives (i.e., more mature human and leadership drives).

Frederick Herzberg's theory isolated two factors correlated with motivation at work.[16] The first—the hygiene, or external, factor—is actually more often associated with dissatisfaction. Elements included in this first factor are company policy, supervision, relationship with boss, work conditions, salary, and relationship with peers. The second factor, which he called the motivators, is correlated with true satisfaction. These motivational factors include achievement, recognition, the work itself, responsibility, advancement, and growth; these represent the sources of positive organizational energy.

Both of these theories suggest that the more mature motives of growth, challenge, achievement, and fulfilling relationships are part of an advanced leader's drive. Yet David McClelland, a noted leadership researcher, added a *need for power* to the basic leadership motives of achievement and affiliation.[17] He found that the best leaders have a natural resonance in positions of authority: They enjoy leading.

McClelland did, however, issue a caution about the dark side of power motivation. He warned against placing those who seem to be motivated for leadership roles, but are actually stuck at lower, less mature levels of a motivational hierarchy. Leaders who are overly concerned with salary and compensation equity, or the trappings of power positions (corner offices, special parking spots, titles, and so on) could eclipse the more productive drives of accomplishment and growth.

Hiring a True Leader

To help explore a candidate's motives to be a leader, examine his or her track record, as reported on a resume or application. Then ask open-ended interview questions about historical accomplishments. A true leader will report pride in accomplishments done by others on the team, or pride in developing others for greater responsibility. Leadership is a vicarious thrill and is actually about getting work done through others, so be wary of a candidate who is overly invested in his or her technical expertise or personal accomplishments; this person may be less motivated to develop as a leader.

A substantial part of a leader's energy is purely physical. The stamina and composure required to lead comes, in part, from a healthy lifestyle. Diet, exercise, and balance provide the vigor required to maintain the energy and positive outlook needed; creativity and energy are not associated with workaholics.[18] Stephen Covey said it best in his book *Seven Habits of Highly Successful People*: Leaders must occasionally stop to *sharpen the saw* to stay effective.[19] For a leader, this means having avocations, friendships, and diversions that provide recreation. In fact, our experience shows six factors that are essential to a balanced and energetic life for a leader:

Vocation: The choice of leadership as a true calling, a genuine desire to do good things through others.

Avocation: Hobbies and pursuits outside of work that are refreshing and recreational.

Relationships: Genuine friendships that provide emotional support.

Materiality: A degree of financial independence that provides security (compensation, insurance, and retirement).

Spirituality: A satisfying worldview that helps put work (and life) in a meaningful context.

Health: The diet, exercise, and rest necessary for the energy required to lead.

Dysfunctional leaders, or leaders who ultimately derail, often have big gaps in one or more of these areas. Professionals who have a mature motivational engine (a balanced life with a personal need to achieve and lead) can get inspiration through truly meaningful work. In an organizational context, this translates into a positive mission, vision, and values that provide identity and meaning.

Organizing and Planning: Get Organized!

This discussion started with competencies considered by some to be the *softer* side of leadership—building relationships, training personnel, exercising power, and finding the right personal motivation to lead. Now let us turn to an absolutely essential *hard* competency: *Organizing and Planning*.

Some authorities make a distinction between leading and managing—and rightfully so. They point out that leading is about *people*: building relationships, creating motivation, and being effective (doing the right things well). Managing, they say, is about *tasks*: namely, being efficient (doing things right).

The *Organizing and Planning* competency is at the heart of good managing. It involves the knowledge and skills to successfully handle the many competing priorities that confront a leader every day. In the past two decades, technology has drastically amplified the need for this competency. Today's leaders are bombarded daily with boatloads of data, e-mails, text messages, and other electronic communications that can easily distract if not handled appropriately.

Time Management

Time is a leader's most precious resource. Its allocation is always a zero sum game: You only get so many effective work hours in a day, and the time you give to one project, person, or idea necessarily subtracts from something else. At the center of the *Organizing and Planning* competency is a difficult question: What is the best use of my time *right now*?

The very best time managers have the *helicopter quality*—they are able to mentally hover above the fray and determine priorities through a continuous process of triaging tasks by urgency and importance.[20] They frequently use a structured process to label tasks and proactively manage priorities (see Table 4.1). The key is to spend as much time as possible in quadrant 2 (very important, not urgent). This allows for the best thinking and results while focusing on the mission-critical issues of the organization. These tasks can be the most difficult to confront, however, and many managers fall into the trap of procrastinating them until the pressure of a deadline forces them to act. Or they may spend too much time in quadrant 3, where it is easy to get caught up with solving easier challenges that are urgent but not all that important.

So how do you determine the relative importance of tasks and issues? Test them in terms of how mission-critical they are. If they impact mission delivery (our fleet is old and in continuous need of repair) or

Table 4.1 Sorting priorities

	VERY URGENT	LESS URGENT
VERY IMPORTANT	1 A Priorities Urgent and important. Act now!	2 B+ Priorities Important but not urgent. The best quadrant to work in; you have time to incubate and consider.
LESS URGENT	3 B− Priorities Urgent but not important.	4 C Priorities Not urgent or important.

compromise a key value (this is an unsafe situation for our employees), then it is important for leadership attention. That is why it is imperative that every leader fully comprehends organizational purpose and operating principles, as well as his or her job description as it supports the mission. Missions vary with organizations, but there are some benchmark values that most organizations share: quality, innovation, service, finance, and safety. Occasionally a value (such as safety) will actually trump the mission.

The very best leaders provide real-time guidance to their organization by paying attention to the highest-priority items on the organizational agenda. For good or bad, if the leader behaves like something is a priority, then followers too will! A leader cannot *not* communicate ... everything speaks.

The Importance of Delegating

The most important time–management tool in a leader's tool kit is delegation. Lee Iacocca, the celebrated Chrysler CEO, famously said that his real leadership breakthrough came as a sales manager, when he realized that leadership was orchestrating the work of others (not doing it himself). When work came his way, he would always ask, 'Is this the best use of my leadership time?' and 'Who else can do this?' Imagine yourself as the orchestra conductor, where you must delegate the task assignments to the musicians. This is the ultimate goal of the strategic leader: orchestrating a team of experts.

By the way, you might be thinking right about now that the best time managers must be workaholics, putting in 16-hour days. But burnout, along with diminishing creativity and effective critical thinking, means it is your *responsibility* as a leader to take breaks for recreation and exercise. We have all felt that surge of energy and creativity that comes with getting away from work for even a day.

Learning *Organizing and Planning* skills is relatively easy—it is the discipline to follow through that often trips up leaders. Experience demonstrates that it is both a leader's vision and enthusiasm coupled with a manager's discipline, organization, and follow up that truly build sustainable organizations.

Hiring the Organized Leader

When looking for a good organizer and planner across a slate of candidates, explore their daily, weekly, and monthly schedules. Look for signs of organization, such as use of their calendar, follow-up lists, preparation, delegation as a habit, evidence of project planning, and so on.

An excellent test for predicting these skills is the in-basket exercise. In this simulation, candidates are faced with the overflowing in-basket of an absent predecessor. They must sort through multiple competing priorities and do so within time constraints. Later the exercise administrator can evaluate their triage logic and efficiency with organizing and planning tools.

While the leadership competencies such as *Influence* and *Relationship Building* might be seen as more compelling, *Organizing and Planning* skills provide the efficiency needed for a sustainable enterprise. Peter Drucker famously refers to *seed corn*—the essential component that must be set aside and reinvested if you hope to have a crop next year. It is the *Organizing and Planning* competency that provides the seed corn in successful organizations.

Communications Skills: A Leader Cannot Not Communicate

The final competency in our discussion, *Communication*, is a collection of skills generally defined by the medium you use to deliver your message. And while the grand eloquence of a superb leader's speech, such as Martin Luther King's "I Have a Dream" speech, is often used to define the epitome of communication competence, the actual definition of good leadership communication is much simpler.

In his classic book *Leaders: Strategies for Taking Charge*, Warren Bennis notes that in his study of 90 exceptional leaders, the true differentiator was not necessarily being good in a particular medium (i.e., public speaking, informal conversation, or writing) but in how the leader is able to frame the message.[21] For example, Bennis notes that a less proficient leader might describe an acre of land in terms of square yards, or hectares, while a true leader would describe an acre as "about the size of a football field" (or *pitch* for you soccer fans). Leaders, then, look for ways to construct their message in a much more accessible way for all potential followers. They tell compelling stories and use parables and images to convey meaning.

Of course, being competent in a full range of media available for communicating a compelling story can amplify your effectiveness as a leader. Our research has isolated five distinct facets to effective leadership communication:[22]

- *Active Listening:* Giving full, proactive attention when others speak. This includes being aware of the importance of all the nonverbal cues that are expected, plus paraphrasing, summarizing, and questioning to ensure full understanding.
- *Communicativeness:* The frequency, volume, and choice of medium that exceptional leaders choose for a message. For example, good leaders know that during times of dramatic change, it is almost impossible to over-communicate. They match the most effective medium to a message and make sure it is transmitted enough times for understanding and ownership. They also convey an eagerness to receive messages from others. They invite communication.
- *Informal Communication:* Conveying information in informal settings clearly and articulately. A leader's communication reputation rests with the ability to connect with people in less formal situations. It is in these situations that messages are perfected and relationships are cemented.
- *Presentation Skills:* Being able to deliver an engaging formal speech to a large gathering. This skill lets you get a message to a multitude quickly.
- *Written Communication:* Writing clearly and concisely. While it is sometimes a neglected skill, good writing represents good thinking, and being able to craft a persuasive argument in written form can help frame a persuasive message delivered later in person.

Communicate Well, Communicate Often

Communication skills do truly distinguish exceptional leadership. Just being intelligent or having a good idea does not qualify you to lead and is not the same as attracting support for your agenda through the contagious enthusiasm generated in superior communication. To lead, you must communicate.

Being a good communicator also means being keenly aware that as a leader, you *are* the message. What is on your calendar, how you present yourself, your attention to detail and myriad other verbal and nonverbal messages are constantly being transmitted whether you intend or not.

It should be noted that direct followers are particularly fond of *Active Listening* in their leaders. An eloquent public speaker can still fall far short as a leader by being inaccessible, unapproachable, or just plain disinterested in his or her direct reports. Informed decisions implemented by committed followers demand involvement, and *Active Listening* ensures that involvement.

Most people rate *Communication Skills* as only moderately difficult to acquire. Even *Presentation Skills*, which in some polls appears as the most feared item by the general population, can be mastered with practice. Our experience has shown, however, that it is not poor communication skills that often derail good leaders, but rather their vanishing motivation to communicate. The hubris that comes with power will often diminish the perceived need to communicate, and the leader will become isolated and less effective. Good leadership requires constant dialogue, and those at the top of an organization must be particularly aware of the general fear of speaking truth to power. They must work hard to stay in touch and remain approachable.

Hiring a Good Communicator

Assessing *Communication Skills* in leadership candidates is fairly simple in the screening interview. The meeting format allows for evaluation of both informal and active listening competence; it is also easy in the panel interview format to require a brief (five-minute) presentation that will allow evaluation of this critical communication skill set. Samples of written work, prepared or spontaneous, are also relatively easily obtained; even e-mail exchanges with candidates can be revealing.

Evaluating a candidate's *Communicativeness* competence does require asking specific behavioral episode questions about historical situations the candidate was involved in that required accelerated information sharing.

For example, find out if a candidate has been in charge of a major organizational change and examine the response in terms of how he or she maintained the dialogue needed to successfully manage the transition.

The Big Plus-One: *Technical and Functional Expertise*

We began this chapter by noting that decades of leadership research has narrowed a much longer list to six competencies that predict effective leadership in a wide variety of settings (the 20 percent of competence that accounts for 80 percent of performance).

But unless you are the CEO of a very diverse conglomerate, there is also a seventh, more particular, competency that is necessary to be an effective leader: *Technical and Functional Expertise.* Having a specialized expertise not only generates personal power for a leader but also provides the content and professional and business context for a legitimate leadership agenda.

Here is an example of how our six competencies combine with expertise to produce exceptional leadership: Decades ago, Sam Walton had the dream "to give ordinary folks the chance to buy the same things as rich people." Walton's vision did not materialize in a vacuum—he was formally educated in business and decided early on to focus on a career in retail, specifically general merchandise. It was this knowledge of retail business that informed Walton's vision and eventually led to the world's largest discount retailer, Walmart.

If we were to rate Walton on our six essential competencies, he would do well on all: He was a driven, passionate leader who knew how to communicate to all levels in his organization. He was a famous organizer—and indeed Walmart is still one of the most efficient organizations on the planet. Walton built a network of vendors and partners that allowed him to rapidly expand his business. But his original dream buried inside of his special retail expertise and was then given life through his exceptional leadership. It is this seventh competency that creates the context for most leaders to form an agenda.

How to Establish an Agenda

Your first step in building a complete agenda is establishing the organizational mission. This statement of purpose is built around a core expertise.

Take, for example, one medical device company's mission: Improve the quality of patient care through the cost-effective monitoring of vital signs and fluid-delivery systems. This assumes expertise in health care, instrumentation, and manufacturing.

To further differentiate your organization, you should add a set of values to your mission. Research reveals that excellent organizations differentiate themselves through quality, innovation, and service.[23] They typically select one of these values to provide even greater identity and distinction. For example, if you are a manufacturer (as our medical instruments company), you must differentiate yourself through a quality product, but you could provide further separation through wonderful customer service or continuous innovation.

The third component of your strategic agenda is a compelling vision. This is a creative statement of a preferred future for the organization. When John F. Kennedy challenged NASA to put a man on the moon by the end of the decade, he was expressing his dream for an agency with the mission of space exploration—but with a compelling benchmark of success. In sum, a complete leadership agenda includes mission, values, and vision that must be framed in an industry context.

Defining Technical Competency

With more than 27,000 different position descriptions listed in the *Dictionary of Occupational Titles*, it is not possible to identify explicit developmental options for a generic *Technical and Functional Expertise* competency.[24] Every technical specialty requires different ability, knowledge, and skill, and each individual comes with a unique learning style.

That said, to learn a functional specialty, you must first make sure to choose an area of expertise and career that truly excites you, then recognize the limits to your abilities. (You may love to play basketball, but at 5 ft 7 in you may have to choose another vocation that interests you, and keep basketball as a hobby.) Next, you need to identify the specific knowledge and skills necessary to being successful. (And remember, you need not have been the star player on your basketball team to be a great coach—what is important is that you played with heart and passion, and that you have the context and credibility of the experience.)

To personally validate this exploration of the Big Six, imagine several of the very best leaders you have ever known (leaders who generate superior results and who are respected, likable, and passionate about what they do). Most likely you experienced them as inspirational, efficient, and effective.

To arrive at that point, they probably started with a specific area of expertise that motivated them and then, through native talent and learning, acquired competence in the Big Six. These competencies provide the necessary foundation for prospecting, recruiting, selecting, training, appraising, and promoting leaders.

The Big Six are a fundamental guide to selecting and developing the people who will contribute to your organization through the challenges of the decades to come.

Questions for Reflection

1. How do the Big Six competencies differ from *Technical and Functional* or *Industry* expertise?
2. What do Human Resources professionals mean when they say that organizations "hire for the hard skills but then fire for the soft skills?"
3. What level on the talent pipeline (i.e., individual contributor, supervisor, manager, and executive) might the Big Six be most important in terms of selection and development?
4. Discuss the Big Six in terms of leadership (focus on people and doing the right things) and management (focus on tasks and doing things right). Which Big Six competencies align with each?
5. Which of the Big Six should you definitely hire for (i.e., the competencies hardest to develop)? What techniques can you use to evaluate job candidates in those competency areas?
6. If you only had time to vet a supervisor candidate on *two* of the Big Six, which two would you choose and why?

CHAPTER 5

Case Studies and Examples

This chapter will bring competency models to life through organizational case studies that exemplify best practice competency applications. Examples of successful uses have been chosen across the key talent management processes of learning and development, performance management, and selection.

Learning and Development Case Studies

The use of competencies as learning criteria to clarify expected work proficiency, improve proficiency in a job, or prepare for a different role is implicit in establishing an organizational competency model. For example, a sales professional aspiring to be the sales manager can readily detect from an organization's competency model that to advance they will need to ensure that they have the knowledge and skill to perform in managerial competencies such as *Delegation*, *Team Management*, *Talent Development (Coaching)*, *Communications*, and *Influence*. Likewise, for the first time, frontline supervisors will also often find themselves in training programs that target these competencies. The following cases are examples of specific successful applications in the area of talent development.

Global Sportswear Company: Teaching Business Competencies Through a Simulation-Based Workshop

The chief financial officer (CFO) of a global apparel and footwear manufacturer identified a need to increase knowledge and skill in several key strategic competencies, including *Business Acumen*, *Decision Making*, *Strategic Thinking*, and *Finance*. These competencies had been previously validated as part of the company's universal competency model and confirmed to be essential to success in mid- and senior-level management roles.

To meet this training need, a custom workshop was developed to provide a full immersion simulation experience that represented a complete business system. This offered participants the opportunity to learn on a *practice field* in a comprehensive business context. The program replicated a seven-year organizational cycle, in which teams of participants assumed leadership roles in the fictitious company and then were challenged to aggressively grow a failing business.

The centerpiece of the program was an intensive, four-day workshop that included the customized computer-based simulation, which was used to emulate the organization's unique matrix design and business model. The agenda included:

Day 1—Welcome from organization's manager or sponsor, team-building exercise, financial acumen lecture, FY01 simulation year, and a financial presentation from the organization's upper-level finance manager.

Day 2—Financial acumen lecture continued, fictitious simulation company overview, decision-making exercises, and break-out team orientation. Homework based on the fictitious company's problems and possible growth opportunity memos.

Day 3—Review previous day's homework and create team decisions on the current business direction; run the simulation model forward three years (FY02, FY03, FY04); debrief in teams the three financial years; and make necessary adjustments.

Day 4—Run the simulation model forward an additional three years (FY05, FY06, and FY07) and get final simulation business results. Team presentations based on results and a program review. A final *bring it home* presentation, which relates the simulation results to real organizational practices, conducted by an upper-level organization manager.

Fifty-two iterations of the program ran over a 10-year period and the workshop ultimately was awarded an American Society of Training and Development (ASTD) Best Practice Citation as a model training event. However, the success of the program rested not just on the positive reaction, but more importantly on a rigorous evaluation plan that used several methods derived from Kirkpatrick's training evaluation model[1] to test competency learning and application. The success of competency learning and transfer to the job was judged on four levels:

Level I: Reaction to training (interesting, informative, valuable)
Level II: Competence (knowledge and skill) gain as a result of training
Level III: Applied and transferred competence
Level IV: Business impact and return on investment (ROI) from improved competence

Level I—Reaction: To assess the participants' reaction to the program, daily and final evaluations were given to them to obtain a perceived value of the program. The daily evaluations rated the pace and degree of participation, and allowed for any additional feedback about the program, while the final evaluation rated the perceived value of every aspect of the program. Driven by valid competencies such as learning objectives (inherent relevance to the work place), experiential learning, and immediate ability to apply the learning, the program reaction remained consistently high throughout the decade the program ran.

Level II—Learning: The second level of evaluation consisted of 44 multiple-choice questions given at the beginning and the end of the program. This exam tested basic to advanced financial knowledge, as well as measured the four learning objectives and competencies that were highlighted. This test was composed of questions regarding the competencies being taught; pre- and postprogram scores revealed statistically significant knowledge gain in competency proficiency across participants.

Level III—Transfer: Throughout the program, the participants were asked to connect what they had learned with how they make decisions in their organization. On the final day of the program, participants developed action plans that they would implement upon returning to work. Those action plans were discussed with, approved by, and continually evaluated by their managers.

Levels IV—Business Impact: To test the business impact of the program, *action learning teams* were formed following the program to address real organizational issues. Teams were composed of interested and expert participants selected from across the simulation teams. Teams were required to track the financial impact (ROI) of their solutions and make a report to the management.

The existence of a valid, universal competency model greatly facilitated program design and delivery. For example, the program was immediately face-valid to participants as they recognized the learning objectives as the competencies they had seen many times in the company's universal model. Participants were motivated to learn, as they recognized the importance of the competencies for future success as they ascended the talent ladder. Training transfer was also assisted because participant supervisors were familiar with program learning objectives (e.g., competencies) and better able to support and coach participants after program completion.

Lipscomb University: A Unique Academic Learning Approach—The Competency-Based Curriculum

Founded in 1891, the Lipscomb University is a private, co-educational, liberal arts university located in Nashville, Tennessee, United States. In 2012, the university introduced a radical innovation to their approach to undergraduate education.[2] Leveraging a well-researched, commercially available competency model, they identified a subset of competencies that were considered essential to job success across a wide range of disciplines. This subset of competencies included *Organizing and Planning, Problem Solving, Relationship Building, Communications Skills,* and *Influence Skills.* The university added all selected competencies to the undergraduate curriculum.

The addition of these competencies would ensure that organizations hiring Lipscomb graduates were not only getting qualified technical professionals such as engineers, nurses, or IT specialists, but were also acquiring new employees who would be certified in the competencies essential for exceptional application of their expertise.

Known as *CORE (customized, outcome based, and relevant evaluation)*, the Lipscomb program features a *Competency Assessment and Development Center* employing a best-practice assessment center.[3]

The Lipscomb *Competency Assessment and Development Center* specifically evaluates the student's proficiency in a subset of competencies that have been found essential for career success in a wide range of organizations and professional specialties. The Lipscomb life skill competency set includes:

- *Active Listening*
- *Problem Solving and Decision Making*

- *Assertiveness (Confidence)*
- *Conflict Management*
- *Relationship Building*
- *Team Player*
- *Change Agility*
- *Influence*
- *Organizing and Planning*
- *Initiative*

Performing in simulations such as leaderless group discussions, in-basket exercises, business cases, role plays, and presentations, participants are evaluated against required proficiency for entry-level job requirements. Students earn competency credits called *badges*, and a probable academic credit, for reaching required performance levels. If participants fall short, then targeted online training and faculty coaching are offered to remedy the gap and ensure that a Lipscomb graduate arrives at the workplace with the complete skillset necessary to succeed in an organizational context. The CORE assessment center began operating in June 2013 and received Southern Association of Colleges and Schools Commission on Colleges (SACSCOC) accreditation in December of that year.

Chemical Bank: A Competency-Based, Survey-Guided Leadership Development Process

Established over 95 years ago and headquartered in Midland, Michigan, Chemical Bank is the largest independently owned Michigan based bank, with over 150 branches across Michigan's Lower Peninsula. As part of an organizational development effort, in 2009, the bank licensed a commercial competency model and customized the competencies to reflect the bank's industry, market, strategy, and culture.

After establishing the model as the common language for talent management, the bank began a survey-guided leadership development effort starting with the top leaders, including the CEO, and cascading through all managers. Guided by the learning principle that it is better to diagnose before you prescribe, the program employed a rigorous multirater survey to provide feedback about how managers were perceived by other employees vis-à-vis an ideal state (i.e., the Chemical Bank competency model).

This popular process has become known as a *360° survey* because participants solicit feedback from all points on the compass surrounding their position on the organization chart.

Multirater 360° surveys have become a best-practice leadership development tool now used in the majority of large American organizations. Typically, a 360° includes the following elements:

- Participating managers identify and invite anonymous feedback on their competence from organizational peers and direct reports. Identified raters are limited to those who have known the participating manager long enough to reliably rate them. Bosses are included, but are not promised anonymity. Once respondents are selected, a third party administers an online survey to those identified. Most 360° surveys solicit feedback from a dozen or more respondents.

- The surveys employ rating scales used to judge and compare perceived proficiency across relevant competencies by the different respondent groups. These quantitative results allow normative comparisons. More robust surveys also solicit open-ended written comments to ensure more complete and specific feedback.

- To ensure that participants understand, own, and act on the survey results, they are packaged into a feedback report and a qualified coach delivers the feedback and helps interpret the report.

- Accountability for any needed improvement surfaced by the survey is ensured through a variety of options, including ongoing coaching, developmental objectives required in performance appraisal documents, follow-up surveys, and informal continuing feedback. Because of issues with politicizing the process and rater accuracy, the vast majority of 360° surveys are used strictly for development. While it is tempting to use 360° feedback for administrative purposes (e.g., informing annual appraisal ratings, or succession management readiness evaluations), experience and research have shown that these applications can damage the 360° reputation and introduce negative power dynamics into the process.

The elements above precisely describe Chemical Bank's 360° process, with the bank strictly adhering to the best practice of using the 360° feedback for development only.[4] The bank's survey process is supervised by a certified external coach, who requests each participant to interpret their own 360° feedback report and present a summary in a feedback discussion. In their summaries, participants contrast current feedback results with previous years' reports and compare their ratings to norms. Each participant also follows up with their different respondent population (i.e., peers, boss, direct reports) to discuss their feedback and learning. The coach also meets with each participant's manager to explain general findings but not to share a complete report or specific ratings. This meeting ensures program transparency and supervisor involvement and improves the likelihood of the supervisor's ongoing support. This supervisory support is essential for a participant's improvement over time. A unique feature of the bank's approach is to also designate a trusted peer for each participant who can be used as a sounding board to discuss results, any needed change, and progress toward goals.

Accountability for follow up and change are linked into the bank's performance appraisal process through required developmental objectives and ratings on competencies. In keeping with best practice, 360° ratings are not transferred to appraisal documents, but participants can measure their progress year-to-year based on subsequent 360° ratings. Another measure of progress is the annual performance rating set on a core set of competencies that every Chemical Bank employee is held accountable for.

It should be noted that at Chemical Bank, the competency model and 360° leadership development process were not just a training initiative, but were also, by introducing the concept of upward feedback, part of a deliberate effort to change organizational culture to encourage more honest, open, and direct feedback. As of time of print, 60 managers had participated in the process at Chemical Bank with a new wave of 360° survey scheduled every 18 months to monitor growth and provide accountability.

The bank has seen improvements in culture and managerial competence, and an unexpected realization of how to better leverage each manager's strengths and weaknesses revealed through the model and the 360° process. By providing a common competency language that is now thoroughly understood across the bank, the competency model and a formal feedback method have resulted in a much more transparent organization with more open and objective feedback. Finally, the introduction of a competency model and 360° evaluations has helped stimulate and objectify a new succession management program at the bank.

Starwood: A Competency-Based Leadership Service Profit Link

Starwood Hotels and Resorts Worldwide Inc., is an American hotel and leisure company headquartered in Stamford, Connecticut. It is one of the world's largest hotel companies and owns, operates, franchises, and manages hotels, resorts, spas, residences, and vacation ownership properties under its nine owned brands, including Sheraton, Westin, St. Regis, Meridian, Aloft, and W. The company owns, manages, or franchises over 1,100 properties employing over 170,000 people around the globe.

Starwood has long leveraged the link between profitability, customer loyalty, and employee engagement as identified in a seminal Harvard Business Review article as the Service Profit Chain model[5] (see Figure 5.1). Starwood original research has also confirmed the link between the quality of company hotel leadership and associate engagement.

To specifically define exceptional leadership at Starwood, the company has implemented a competency architecture known as the *Win with Talent* competency model. Among other applications, *Win with Talent* competencies provide the criteria for a biennial 360° survey-guided development experience for leadership teams on Starwood properties. These hotel leadership teams, or executive committees (ECs), include the general manager, and possibly directors of sales, food & beverage, finance, housekeeping, operations, and engineering, depending on the property size.

To demonstrate the efficacy of this leadership development program, Starwood conducted research that proved the link between improved leadership competence as judged by 360° survey ratings and improved

Figure 5.1 *Starwood service profit chain*

property financial performance. First, the research verified the correlation between higher EC leadership 360° ratings and higher associate engagement scores as measured by a regular engagement survey called StarVoice. The study then established the connection between exceptionally engaged employees and improved customer satisfaction. Finally, research over time revealed a clear relationship between elevated engagement scores and property financial performance as indicated by average daily room rates and hotel revenue performance against a competitive set.

The research has advanced to actually identifying the specific competencies that property leaders *must* be proficient in to begin this positive cascade. For example, the competency *Active Listening* practiced by leaders can be a key driver in associate satisfaction and ultimately in guest satisfaction.

The uniform *Win with Talent* competency model used across Starwood has thus allowed the company to optimize its talent management tools and processes, and ultimately produce more efficient and effective human resources systems.

Competencies in Performance Management

Competency models help provide individual role clarity, which is the fundamental building block in performance management. Setting expectations up-front establishes the ideal state for the job, and allows for legitimate feedback, both positive and corrective, along the way. As performance management systems shift toward a more positive and developmental orientation, competencies become more important in defining and developing job competence.

Art Supply Company: Competency-Based Performance Management System

A medium-sized east coast art supply manufacturer scrapped their performance management system and began designing from scratch a *Performance Recognition System* that would leverage a new universal competency model. Company managers were invited to a workshop to

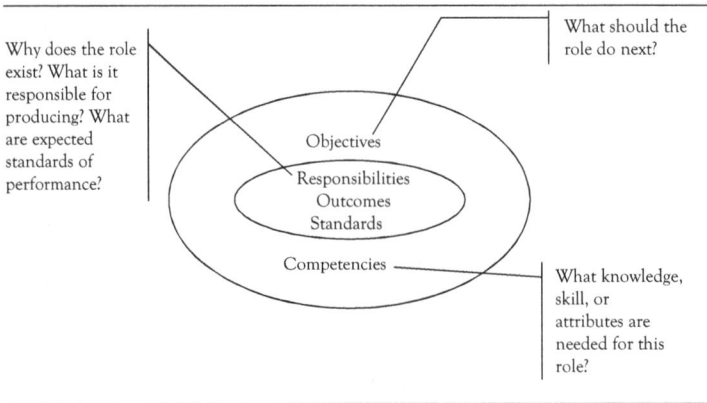

Figure 5.2 Job model

provide input to the new design. Products of the workshop included a new job model for the company to conceptualize each role.

A complete conceptualization of any individual role at the company is absolutely essential to successful performance management. Managers should begin the performance recognition process with a clear understanding of the role in question. A clear model provides:

- Clear role definition, responsibilities, standards, authority, and expected results
- Motivating objectives to focus energy
- Specific definitions of the knowledge, skill, or attributes needed to perform

Once a clear job model had been established to clarify company roles, a position description (called a *Success Profile* by the company) was generated as the foundation for setting role expectations and managing performance.

This example of a success profile (Figure 5.3) not only clarified roles and responsibilities but it also served as the basis for setting business and personal development objectives for each manager. Objective accomplishment was required to qualify for the company's variable pay plan. Developmental objectives were driven by the company's competency model and ensured focused development necessary for exceptional performance in the assigned role.

Job title			Job reports to:		
Job band:					
Status: exempt or non-Exempt full-time or part time					
Prepared by:			Approved by:		
Job code		Department			Date prepared
Mission: A motivating description, in one sentence, of why the position exists. The purpose of the job. How the job adds value:					
Core accountabilities: Up to ten (preferably 5-7) principle responsibilities with expected results. List percentage weight (10% minimum) for each					
% of Job		Key accountabilities and responsibilities			Outcome and result
Core job competencies: List up to 10 competencies from the company's Leadership and Management Success Profile (job-specific: technical and universal) most required to achieve the core accountabilities for the position (the *how*). Encompass the key dimensions of overall competencies that collectively distinguish superior from less than superior job performance: knowledge, skills, self-image, values, traits and motives. For appraisal purposes, this is the *short list* of differentiating competencies. For career development applications, assessment against a larger dictionary of competencies is important, as long as each position has a unique set of core competencies.					
Key objectives: The major business objectives that this role must accomplish in the next reporting period. Personal developmental objectives that would enhance individual performance in this role.					
Business objectives (2–4)					By when?
Developmental objectives (2–4)					By when?
Learning opportunities: Key job assignments and accomplishments that constitute the *lessons of experience* for a given position; i.e., what one can expect to learn as a result of successfully performing the job. In the aggregate, this portfolio of experiences represents the essential building blocks for long-term career growth at *The Company*					
Cross-departmental business management assignments (regional, business unit, functional).					
Cross-cultural assignments					
Strategic planning assignments for new business growth and development					
Nature and Scope					
Number of reports (direct or dotted)		Revenue and profit accountabilities			Annual operating budget
Physical and technical environment: List any specific tools, technologies, substances, hazards and/or protective equipment needed to perform job. Also list percentage of time spent on each.					
Risk management and liability impact					
Position in organizational chart, including immediate manager (direct or dotted), others reporting to immediate manager, and others reporting to this position.					
Experience requirements: the prerequisite job-related qualifications for this position, such as education, industry, product, or service background, professional training and certification(s), staff development accomplishments, administrative experience, etc.					
Education and work experience					

Figure 5.3 Success profile

Competencies in Talent Selection

Superfeet Worldwide: Competency-Based President Selection

Superfeet Worldwide, a global consumer products organization, was facing a change of its president. The chairman of the board of directors chose an executive search and talent management firm to partner with in the selection process. Having made judgment errors in past appointments, they were acutely aware of the need for good hiring practices that would focus on critical job requirements and assess all candidates in the same fair, consistent, and objective manner.

The first step was to look at the competencies that would define job success. To establish these success criteria they used a commercially available competency model that had identified 41 competencies necessary for effective performance. Using the model's competency cards, the Executive Search Committee (ESC) sorted through the competencies to identify a subset of key competencies essential to the role of president at Superfeet. Over the course of rich dialog, six competencies were determined to be core competencies for use in the selection process. Those six were then used to create a position success profile, which was fleshed out with core accountabilities and key objectives in the role.

The external search team was given the success profile and told to use the six competencies as the foundation of their search criteria. In collaboration with the ESC, a series of behavioral episode interview questions was developed for each of the six competencies. To ensure the interview would be structured around the competencies, a proficiency scale for each competency was developed and integrated into the evaluation form.

Once the external search partner provided a sufficient number of screened candidates, the ESC moved forward to onsite interviews. Specific training was provided to the members of the interview board. Focus was placed on:

- Competency definition and understanding
- Ways of soliciting behavioral evidence from application documents, during an interview, and from reference checks
- Ways to avoid rater bias

As a strong selection process based on those competencies was considered essential to the role of president, Superfeet was able to identify the individual most likely to satisfy the success profile they had created. After 12 months in the role, the executive team reported significant progress and impact from the new president. The president exceeded the requirements for the role, and his performance reflected strengths in the six essential competencies. Additionally, he had established credibility with the executive team and had established the first strategic business plan for the organization. Lastly, the new president had built rapport with key customers to continue driving increased revenues.

With cases drawn from a wide variety of successful competency applications hopefully both the utility and credibility of competency models have been reinforced. It is interesting to note that different organizations first applied their models in an area of immediate need (e.g., more transparent leadership, more innovative approach to learning, culture change, and so on). Remedying this immediate problem established a beachhead for model expansion once the application had proven itself and gained a positive reputation. Whether by design or happenstance, these successful applications employed positive change management principles.

Questions for Reflection

1. Describe a competency application in selection, development and performance.
2. How have you seen competencies applied in your organization?
3. What applications highlighted in this chapter might be combined to ensure exceptional leadership competence?
4. Describe how one organization used the service profit chain to prove the financial utility of competency models.

Notes

Chapter 1

1   Murray (1948).
2   Schein (1990a).
3   McClelland (1973).
4   Shippmann et al. (2000).
5   Campion et al. (2011).
6   Griffiths (2009).
7   Griffiths (2009).
8   Campion et al. (2011).
9   Thornton and Byham (1982).
10 Rosier (1997).
11 Lawshe (1975).
12 Howard and Bray (1990).
13 Arthur et al. (2003).

Chapter 2

1   Ames and Flynn (2007).
2   Chamberlain (2009).

Chapter 3

1   Carter (2014).
2   Dowell (2010).
3   Ennis (2008).
4   Draganidis and Mentzas (2006).
5   McDaniel et al. (1994).
6   U.S. Office of Personnel Management (2008).
7   International Task Force on Assessment Center Guidelines (2009).
8   Wanous (1992).
9   Smither (1998).
10 Spencer and Spencer (2008).
11 Spencer and Spencer (2008).
12 Spencer and Spencer (2008).
13 French and Bell (1999).

14   Nelson (2014).
15   Washington (2009).
16   Washington et al. (2011).

Chapter 4

1   Griffiths (2010).
2   Barling, Slater, and Kelloway (2000).
3   George (2000).
4   Einarsen, Aasland, and Skogstad (2007).
5   Reiter-Palmon and Illies (2004).
6   Hausknecht, Rodda, and Howard (2009).
7   Von Oech (1998).
8   Myers and Myers (1995).
9   Gladwell (2007).
10   Babcock-Roberson and Strickland (2010).
11   French and Raven (1959).
12   Mehrabian (1971).
13   McClelland and Burnham (2003).
14   Schein (1990b).
15   Maslow (1943).
16   Herzberg (1987).
17   McClelland and Burnham (2003).
18   Quick et al. (2006).
19   Covey (2012).
20   Newell (1989).
21   Bennis and Nanus (1985).
22   Griffiths (2010).
23   Peters and Watermon (1982).
24   Cain and Treiman (1981).

Chapter 5

1   Kirkpatrick and Kirkpatrick (1994).
2   Klein-Collins and Olson (2014).
3   "Guidelines and Ethical Considerations for Assessment Center Operations"
     (2009).
4   Rogers, Rogers, and Mettay (2011).
5   Heskett et al. (1994).

References

Ames, D.R., and F.J. Flynn. 2007. "What Breaks a Leader: The Curvilinear Relation Between Assertiveness and Leadership." *Journal of Personality and Social Psychology* 92, no. 2, p. 307.

Arthur, W., E.A. Day, T.L. McNelly, and P.S. Edens. 2003. "A Meta-analysis of the Criterion-Related Validity of Assessment Center Dimensions." *Personnel Psychology* 56, no. 1, pp. 125–53.

Babcock-Roberson, M.E., and O.J. Strickland. 2010. "The Relationship Between Charismatic Leadership, Work Engagement, and Organizational Citizenship Behaviors." *The Journal of Psychology* 144, no. 3, pp. 313–26.

Barling, J., F. Slater, and E.K. Kelloway. 2000. "Transformational Leadership and Emotional Intelligence: An Exploratory Study." *Leadership & Organization Development Journal* 21, no. 3, pp. 157–61.

Bennis, W., and B. Nanus. 1985. *Leaders: The Strategies for Taking Charge.* NY: Harper & Row Publishers.

Cain, P.S., and D.J. Treiman. 1981. "The Dictionary of Occupational Titles as a Source of Occupational Data." *American Sociological Review* pp. 253–78.

Campion, M.A., A.A. Fink, B.J. Ruggeberg, L. Carr, G.M. Phillips, and R.B. Odman. 2011. "Doing Competencies Well: Best Practices in Competency Modeling." *Personnel Psychology* 64, no. 1, pp. 225–62.

Carter, L. 2014. "Drive Business Strategy by Integrating Talent Decisions." *T&D* 68, no. 6, pp. 76–77.

Chamberlain, J.M. 2009. Disentangling Aggressiveness and Assertiveness Within the MMPI-2 PSY-5 Aggressiveness Scale [PhD dissertation]. Kent State University.

Covey, S. 2012. *The Seven Habits of Highly Successful People.* Fireside/Simon & Schuster.

Dowell, B.E. 2010. "Managing Leadership Talent Pools." In *Strategy-Driven Talent Management: A Leadership Imperative*, 399–438. San Francisco, CA: John Wiley & Sons.

Draganidis, F., and G. Mentzas. 2006. "Competency Based Management: A Review of Systems and Approaches." *Information Management & Computer Security* 14, no. 1, pp. 51–64.

Einarsen, S., M.S. Aasland, and A. Skogstad. 2007. "Destructive Leadership Behaviour: A Definition and Conceptual Model." *The Leadership Quarterly* 18, no. 3, pp. 207–16.

Ennis, M.R. 2008. "Competency Models: A Review of the Literature and the Role of the Employment and Training Administration (ETA)." Office of Policy Development and Research, Employment and Training Administration, U.S. Department of Labor.

French, J.R.P. Jr., and B. Raven. 1959. "The Bases of Social Power". In *Group Dynamics*, eds. D. Cartwright and A. Zander. NY: Harper and Row.

French, W.L., and C.H. Bell Jr. 1999. *Organization Development: Behavioral Science Interventions for Organization Improvement.* Upper Saddle River, NJ: Prentice Hall.

George, J.M. 2000. "Emotions and Leadership: The Role of Emotional Intelligence." *Human Relations* 53, no. 8, pp. 1027–55.

Gladwell, M. 2007. *Blink: The Power of Thinking Without Thinking.* Hachette Digital, Inc.

Griffiths, B. 2009. Taking the Mystery Out of Talent Management: A Research Report in Support of Polaris® Competency Models and 360° Multi-rater Measurements. Organization Systems International.

Griffiths, B. 2010. *The Big Six Leadership Competencies. Best Practices* (newsletter), Red Flash Group.

"Guidelines and Ethical Considerations for Assessment Center Operations." 2009. *International Journal of Selection and Assessment* 17, no.3.

Hausknecht, J.P., J. Rodda, and M.J. Howard. 2009. "Targeted Employee Retention: Performance-Based and Job-Related Differences in Reported Reasons for Staying." *Human Resource Management* 48, no. 2, pp. 269–88.

Herzberg, F.I. September/October 1987. "One More Time: How Do You Motivate Employees?" *Harvard Business Review* 65, no. 5, pp. 109–20.

Heskett, J.L., T.O. Jones, G.W. Loveman, W.E. Sasser, and L.A. Schlesinger. 1994. "Putting the Service Profit Chain to Work." *Harvard Business Review*, pp. 164–74.

Howard, A., and D.W. Bray. 1990. "Predictions of Managerial Success over Long Periods of Time: Lessons from the Management Progress Study." In *Measures of Leadership*, eds. K.E. Clark, M.B. Clark, and R. Robert, 113–30. West Orange, NJ: Leadership Library of America.

International Task Force on Assessment Center Guidelines. 2009. "Guidelines and Ethical Considerations for Assessment Center Operations." *International Journal of Selection and Assessment* 17, no. 3, pp. 243–53.

Kirkpatrick, D.L., and J.D. Kirkpatrick. 1994. *Evaluating Training Programs.* Berrett-Koehler Publishers.

Klein-Collins, R., and R. Olson. 2014. Customized, Outcome-based, Relevant Evaluation (CORE) at Lipscomb University. Council for Adult and Experiential Learning (CAEL).

Lawshe, C.H. 1975. "A Quantitative Approach to Content Validity1." *Personnel Psychology* 28, no. 4, pp. 563–75.

Maslow, A.H. 1943. "A Theory of Human Motivation." *Psychological Review* 50, no. 4, p. 370.

McClelland, D.C. 1973. "Testing for Competence Rather than for 'Intelligence.'" *American Psychologist* 28, no. 1, p. 1.

McClelland, D.C., and D.H. Burnham. 2003. "Power Is the Great Motivator." *Harvard Business Review* 81, no. 1, pp. 117–126.

McDaniel, M.A., D.L. Whetzel, F.L. Schmidt, and S.D. Maurer. 1994. "The Validity of Employment Interviews: A Comprehensive Review and Meta-analysis." *Journal of Applied Psychology* 79, no. 4, p. 599.

Mehrabian, A. 1971. *Silent Messages*. 1st ed. Belmont, CA: Wadsworth

Murray, H.A. 1948. *Assessment of Men: Selection of Personnel for the Office of Strategic Services*. Rinehart.

Myers, I.B., and P.B. Myers. 1995. *Gifts Differing: Understanding Personality Type*. Davies-Black Publishing.

Nelson, B. 2014. "The Data on Diversity." *Communications of the ACM* 57, no. 11, pp. 86–95. Business Source Premier, EBSCOhost (accessed March 8, 2015).

Newell, C. 1989. *City Executives: Leadership Roles, Work Characteristics, and Time Management*. SUNY Press.

Peters, T., and R.H. Watermon. 1982. *Search of Excellence*. Harper Collins.

Quick, J.C., M. Macik-Frey, D.A. Mack, N. Keller, D.A. Gray, and C.L. Cooper. 2006. "Healthy Leaders, Healthy Organizations: Primary Prevention and the Positive Effects of Emotional Competence." In *Stress and Quality of Working Life: Current Perspectives in Occupational Health*, eds. A.M. Rossi, P.L. Perrewe, and S.L. Sauter. Greenwich, CT: Information Age Publishing.

Reiter-Palmon, R., and J.J. Illies. 2004. "Leadership and Creativity: Understanding Leadership from a Creative Problem-Solving Perspective." *The Leadership Quarterly* 15, no. 1, pp. 55–77.

Rogers, E., C.W. Rogers, and W. Mettay. 2011. "Improving the Pay-Off for 360° Feedback." *Human Resources Management*. pp. 44–54.

Rosier, R., ed. 1997. *Competency Model Handbook*. Linkage.

Schein, E.H. 1990a. *Career Anchors: Discovering Your Real Values*. San Diego: University Associates.

Schein, E.H. 1990b. "Organizational Culture." *American Psychologist* 45, no. 2.

Shippmann, J.S., R.A. Ash, M. Batjtsta, L. Carr, L.D. Eyde, B. Hesketh, J. Kehoe, K. Pearlman, E.P. Prien, and J.I. Sanchez. 2000. "The Practice of Competency Modeling." *Personnel Psychology* 53, no. 3, pp. 703–40.

Smith, M.J. 1975. *When I Say No, I Feel Guilty: for Managers and Executives.* Volumes I and II. Bantam.

Smither, R.D. 1998. *The Psychology of Work and Human Performance.* Longman.

Spencer, L.M., and P.S.M. Spencer. 2008. *Competence at Work Models for Superior Performance.* John Wiley & Sons.

Thornton, G.C., and W.C. Byham. 1982. *Assessment Centers and Managerial Performance.* NY: Academic Press.

U.S. Office of Personnel Management. 2008. Structured Interviews: A Practical Guide. Washington, DC: US Office of Personnel Management.

Von Oech, R. 1998. *A Whack on the Side of the Head.* Warner Books, Inc.

Wanous, J.P. 1992. *Organizational Entry: Recruitment, Selection, Orientation, and Socialization.* Reading, MA: Addison-Wesley.

Washington, E.G. November/December 2009. "Diversity Is Not a Numbers Game." *Diversity Executive* pp. 27, 55.

Washington, E., J. Johnson, B. McCloskley, P. Toliver, M. Simon, R. Simon, M. Ford, and C. Washington. 2011. *TCRP Report 148 Practical Resources for Recruiting Minorities for Chief Executive Officers at Public Transportation Agencies.* Washington, D.C.: Transportation Research Board.

Index

Announcing the Business Expert Press Digital Library

Concise e-books business students need for classroom and research

This book can also be purchased in an e-book collection by your library as

- a one-time purchase,
- that is owned forever,
- allows for simultaneous readers,
- has no restrictions on printing, and
- can be downloaded as PDFs from within the library community.

Our digital library collections are a great solution to beat the rising cost of textbooks. E-books can be loaded into their course management systems or onto students' e-book readers. The **Business Expert Press** digital libraries are very affordable, with no obligation to buy in future years. For more information, please visit **www.businessexpertpress.com/librarians**. To set up a trial in the United States, please email **sales@businessexpertpress.com**.

www.ingramcontent.com/pod-product-compliance
Lightning Source LLC
Chambersburg PA
CBHW060242230326
41458CB00094B/1410